# the yachtsman's mate's guide

by Margie Livingston

YACHTING/BOATING BOOKS · ZIFF-DAVIS PUBLISHING COMPANY

NEW YORK

# Contents

# Contents

# Foreword

Boating is a family sport, to be shared, and savored by all. But the sea can be a strict disciplinarian, particularly to the unprepared, and your enjoyment will be in direct relationship to the crew's ability to meet the challenges.

Competency in *all* aspects of seagoing life is not usually attainable by a single person—in fact, the most effective crews, and the happiest families, are those in which the acquired skills complement each other. Adam Smith's theory of the division of labor, while sometimes considered old-fashioned by shorebound advocates, has a long and successful tradition at sea. This is not to discourage any family member from developing skills in every facet of the art—quite the contrary, the learning process is one of the best parts of the sport —but rather to suggest that each concentrate first on the things he or she does best. There can be only one captain and one mate, and the tasks are equally important, even though the role of the mate often plays second lead in accounts which tend to glorify the skipper's position of authority.

This book will reveal the many skills demanded of the mate and help you to attain them, thereby contributing in a major way to your families' and friends' enjoyment afloat. I say, "Hats off to the Mate!" I hope you develop into one as good as the author who condescends to sail with me.

STAFFORD CAMPBELL
Noroton, Connecticut

# Introduction

Most of the earth's surface is covered with water and it is natural, perhaps, that we are lured to the sea. Since history has been recorded, the sagas of men and their ships have been told and retold but with little mention of the women who were partners in the planning and often companions during the voyages.

Yesterday's seagoing woman who chose to leave shorebound security to accompany her captain was poorly prepared for ocean life. She was given none of the seagoing apprenticeship available to young men of those times. Verbal counsel from a mariner friend was sometimes available, but more likely was a sink-or-swim exposure to the rigors of the sea *on* board *at* sea. During a two- to six-year voyage as the only woman aboard, she faced months of lonely passages in doldrums and hurricanes, to make a landfall in hazardous uncharted waters, to meet—not the welcoming dancing maidens of romantic novels but grim warriors in battle regalia.

Despite the lack of preparation, many of these women adapted well to sea life. Some are remembered for their heroic behavior in times of crisis. Minerva Ann McCrimmin, young daughter of the captain on board the Great Lakes schooner *David Andrew,* stood at the helm during a wild Lake Ontario squall, and, while the crew doused the sails, calmly beached the ship to safety. Catherine Mayhew, wife of the captain of the whaling bark *Powhatan,* nursed the captain and crew through a smallpox epidemic on board, and navigated the ship competently from New Zealand to the United States. The Countess of Roth manned the tiller to steer her lifeboat to safety after the sinking of the *Titanic.*

Today's woman may never have to face the drama of plague and shipwreck, but, like her seagoing female ancestors, she is an active participant in marine activities; yet, other than cookbooks, there is still, today, very little written specifically to help her prepare for boating life. Forsaking a safe and orderly home ashore, she is expected to adjust immediately to a spartan seafaring world of cramped and crowded quarters, climatic extremes—even a foreign vocabulary—with her only sea training, a crash course aboard delivered by an impatient skipper during a hasty weekend. From novices who were indoctrinated in this fashion come these admissions: "I cry a lot," "I could kill the skipper," "I'm all left feet and stupid."

It is time now to dry the tears, cooperate with the skipper, and use your properly aligned feet and clever Homo sapiens brain. This book is dedicated to you and all mates—innocent landlubbers, sophomore trainees, and seasoned mariners—with the hope that you will gain knowledge, confidence, and enthusiasm for the best of all experiences, small boat cruising.

Whether you are a small boat partner, co-owner, charterer, guest or crew member, your title is "mate," defined by Webster as "one who associates with another . . . partner . . . pal," or less diplomatically in *The Naval Officer's Guide,* as an "officer . . . ranking below the captain." These are skeletal terms for a full-bodied job involving, in a small vessel, the combined tasks of Executive Officer, Mess Treasurer, and even Ensign Pulver's "Laundry and Morale Officer." Successful execution of these duties marks the difference between indifferent and enjoyable boat living.

It takes time to become an experienced mate, and there is no substitute for live-aboard training. Boating skills, learned in theory, may bring stage fright to the budding mariner when the moment of practice arrives. We all experience that pang of insecurity and inadequacy associated with a new venture. But, *you,* today's woman, however humble your attitude or meager your seagoing experience, are well prepared for your new role. In the credit column is your shore background of physical fitness, home management, financial skills and successful association with friends, family, and business colleagues. Add the attributes of intellectual curiosity and the spirit of adventure which brought you into the boating scene and you are well on your way to making the transition from shore to sea. You can be a capable mariner, a major contributor to your boat, and, in Navy lingo, add to the "comfort and contentment of the crew."

Of paramount importance is your partnership with your skipper. On your boat, as on every boat that plies the seas, the captain is the boss. Because he alone has the ultimate responsibility for the safety of his vessel and crew, his decisions must be respected by everyone on board. It's easy to be a pal, but not so comfortable to accept secondary rank in today's egalitarian society, particularly when you have established patterns of balanced partnership ashore. To many of us, the "Yes, sir" response is unfamiliar, if not downright demeaning. It can be a bitter blow to our pride to accept this seemingly archaic chain of command, and we sometimes demonstrate a muleheadedness unbecoming to our title of mate. I flinch at the recollection of some of my own lapses, in particular, an early docking maneuver at a crowded marina where I ignored the instructions of my skipper. Instead, I "did my own thing," and with my own inventive knots and loops created a perfect spider web that snarled our sloop sideways in the slip, bringing merriment to the faces of the Sunday spectators, red rage to the face of the skipper, and egg all over mine.

In learning any new sport or skill, there are moments of frustration. Boating is no exception. There will be trying times and times to test your patience and ingenuity . . . and sanity. In certain instances you will be tempted to turn the whole project over to the sea birds, who are properly equipped and cleverly trained for a maritime life. But, keep your cool, and most of all, your sense of humor. Venture forth, practice your trade, and follow the suggestions in this book to become an accomplished mariner—not in one night like a Cinderella—but, never again a landlubber. So, off with the glass slipper and on with the deck shoes, Mate. Welcome aboard!

# 1. Shakedown

Unlike some sports which may be learned deliberately and privately—tennis serves on a back court or golf swings on a far tee—boating is a public spectator sport with the world gathered around to watch your trials in docking and maneuvering. Your boat and the boats around you are moving targets; the whole scene is like a dress rehearsal in front of an audience—and you haven't even read the script.

We all have the Walter Mitty visions: "Starboard tack across the starting line, first in the fleet, with radiant mate at the helm . . ." (Have you ever been swept over the line backward, sails aback, sheets in snarls, mate in tears?) More Mitty: "Entering the harbor before the admiring gaze of the anchored fleet—skipper to the mate, 'Well done, dear' . . ." (Or the sunset silhouette of

a boat hard aground, anchor line in knots, clarion call from the captain to the mate, "I said 'reverse,' block-head!")

## Instructions in Seamanship

How to turn Mitty fiction into fact? How can you become an able, willing, and competent mariner? Before even leaving the harbor, you can get a good head start by joining classes in seamanship in your community. The U.S. Coast Guard Auxiliary, with posts in most large cities and boating communities in the U.S., offers an introductory course entitled "Boating Skills and Seamanship," consisting of two hours of classroom lectures once a week for a period of twelve weeks. Information about schedules and meeting places may be obtained from your nearest U.S. Coast Guard recruiting station.

The U.S. Power Squadron, a private institution with nationwide offices, provides classes in safe boating. Their introductory course consists of twenty-four hours of lecture and demonstration, conducted in two-hour class sessions once a week. Your local newspaper, radio station, boating center, or marine store should have specific information about the squadron in your area.

Classes of both organizations are held after working hours, free of charge, with only a modest fee for text or reading material. The few hours that you devote to class lectures and homework will pay dividends later when you put your new skills into practice. An incidental bonus to the acquisition of boating lore is the introduction to other seafaring enthusiasts in your community.

## Swimming

Downeasters in Maine and Nova Scotia fish the icy waters in small boats and boast bravely that they can't swim a stroke and never will. These gutsy fishermen have my admiration. However, to be a useful participant in boating, I recommend that everyone learn to swim well enough to remain afloat (and calm) in choppy seas in the event of a sudden dunking. Perhaps your cruising ground will include those northern waters where swimming is a test of polar bear lineage, but more likely, there will be protected coves and serene harbors where a pre-breakfast dip, noon soak, or evening bathe is a joyful adjunct to boating.

If you have been fortunate enough to grow up by a lake or seashore and have learned to swim from early childhood, you take your swimming skill for granted. You have respect for, not fear of, the water and your adjustment to boating will probably be easy. On the other hand, if you are a nonswimmer, lacking early exposure to water sports, you may be timid or uneasy on narrow boat decks and in small dinghies, even in the secure cabin or cockpit of a heeling sailboat. A crew member who has a constant fear of falling overboard will probably never become a capable mariner.

Many adults are deterred from swimming instruction because they envision a beginner's class of pool frolics with seven-year-olds. Most community pools, clubs, and beach areas offer introductory courses for *adults only*— low-key lessons paced for gradual adjustment to the water with emphasis on attaining confidence among peers. If you need encouragement in joining such a swimming class, take a cue from local citizens who attended the Adult Novice Swimming Class at our YMCA recently. Ninety-five percent of the members who entered the season as embarassed or fearful nonswimmers completed the course as "graduates." Many have progressed to advanced techniques in style and distance swimming, and all have a delightful new sport to enjoy for the rest of their lives.

# First Aid

If you plan to cruise offshore or in uninhabited areas, you or some other crew member should know the basics of first aid. Although most of your boat ministrations will be aspirin and sunburn cream, you will wisely prepare for unforeseen accidents which can happen at sea out of range of medical advice and facilities. The American Red Cross offers a course called "Standard First Aid and Personal Safety," consisting of twenty-one to thirty hours of lectures and demonstration. The weekly classes are free except for the text, which is a valuable addition to any medicine chest, aboard or at home. If you can't spare time for the entire course, attend the session on artificial respiration, or learn the techniques from your local police, fire station, or ambulance unit. *Everyone* engaged in water sports should know how to administer emergency resuscitation to revive a victim from possible drowning.

# Nautical Terms

Last in your shore study is the nautical vocabulary. It is historic, colorful and universal. The expressions "fore and aft," "port and starboard," "galley and head," and other seaman's lingo, are bewildering at first to the layman or landlubber, but are as essential to the successful operation of a seagoing vessel as surgeons' terminology is to hospital procedures. Specific nautical terms are used to describe every part of a ship or boat, and to simplify commands or responses when handling boating gear. To advise the skipper "That rope out back is loose!" when the dinghy painter is improperly cleated is clever observation on your part, but may result in a driftaway tender by the time the puzzled skipper has interpreted your message. It probably won't earn you any gold stars at the evening gam. Tuck all the funny new phrases in your verbal ditty bag and enjoy the linguistics of the boating world. To help you on your way, all the nautical terms used in this book are defined in the glossary.

## Sea Trials

You have done all your shore homework. Now is the time to put theory into practice. Yachting ads show the skipper conning the dream boat through sparkling seas with the mate lounging decoratively in the cockpit—perhaps passing the canapés at sunset. What the ads don't show is the working mate who sets and douses sails, steers the boat in difficult seas, and can cook up a storm *in* a storm.

You should know your boat from stem to stern. The initial sight of deck fittings, unfamiliar hardware, and impressive instrument panels may frighten you. However, a modern kitchen is equipped with complicated appliances too. If you are able to operate your kitchen aids efficiently, you can understand the functioning of the gear aboard a boat.

Your first exposure to boating may be as a spectator. If you are lucky enough to start your training among experienced mariners, observe carefully and ask thoughtful questions when the maneuver or terminology is not clear. Most able seafarers are hams at heart and love to talk shop. It will be apparent to you that the time for queries and answers is not in the middle of a complicated "all-hands" sail change or traffic jam, but later—with your boat notebook in hand—to jot memos which will serve as a reminder on your next voyage.

If you must start your sea trials as an active participant, you can avoid the misery that has stricken other budding mariners by trying your helmsmenship on a calm day with light winds under the guidance of a competent *patient* instructor; on those first days of sea trials leave the nervous guests and offspring at home. Perhaps your skipper is your true love, closest chum, or next of kin with the added laudable attributes of a tolerant knowledgeable tutor. If so, your training sessions will be easy—cheers to you both. Sometimes, however, this close relationship kindles sparks between teacher and student; if so, you would be better advised to start your boating lessons with someone who will be more objective about your progress and (because we tend to be a little sassy with our kinfolk) to whom you might be more respectful.

On your first shorthanded sea trial, take time to become acquainted with the boat gear which will be your responsibility before you leave the dock or mooring. Step-by-step explanations by the skipper will ward off misunderstanding at the start. For example, as you depart, know the order for removing lines and fenders and, once under way, be able to stow this gear in the exact orderly fashion expected by the skipper. You may be surprised to find that this seaman who casually wears mismatched socks ashore will insist on docking lines coiled in perfect symmetry. No matter how unreasonable these instructions may seem to you, follow them to the letter, and discuss the whys and wherefores later in a quiet interval.

The rule of orderly stowage applies particularly to all boat safety gear. Learn the location of fire extinguishers, life jackets and emergency pumps, and know how to use them. Be able to locate signalling gear such as horns, bells, and spotlights. If your boat is equipped with a radiotelephone, learn the correct procedure for its use in an emergency.

Every good seaman has a repertoire of nautical knots. The names of some of these alone will lure you to the world of boating. "Barrel sling," "double twofold overhand bend," "man-o'-war sheepshank," "Tom Fool's sheepshank" are some of the picturesque knots for the collector. You only need to know a few essential knots, but you must be able to execute them quickly under all conditions. In an early U.S. Power Squadron course, tying a bowline behind the back was a mandatory skill. In my boating experience that acrobatic skill has never been needed, and I doubt that it will in yours. Yet the ability to tie a fast bowline or clove hitch will be useful every day of your cruising life.

You will be a more efficient mariner if you understand the technical apparatus aboard your boat—the engine or auxiliary, electrical system, water pumps, galley stove, radio equipment, marine toilet. If you are not a mechanical wizard, keep careful memos in your boat notebook. My procedure list for commissioning and decomissioning our boat is as useful to me today as it was twelve years ago.

A boat galley is a cleverly arranged miniature of a home kitchen, so simple that you may question the need for all those special appliances at home. The operation of a galley stove, however, may be different from that of your kitchen range. If you are unfamiliar with the procedure for filling and lighting an alcohol or kerosene stove or with the safety checks of butane or propane, enlist the help of an experienced sea cook before you light off the first time.

The final step of your sea trials is the shakedown (actual practice under way), taking the helm, steering a compass course, operating the controls of the boat under power or sail. Just as in your first automobile practice, it will take time to develop a "feel" for your vessel. It takes many hours at the helm under all conditions to become a proficient boat-handler—don't be discouraged on your first trip.

If you have been able to complete your initial lesson in favorable weather, your boating career is off to a fine start. If, however, the gentle zephyrs have turned to a tempest—and this is the challenge of boating—your sea trial may include more evolutions than you and your skipper had planned. In a shorthanded situation, *you* are essential to the boat. Keep your cool, follow the instructions of the captain to the best of your ability, save your questions for the quiet anchorage, and celebrate winning your first test at sea.

# Rowing

Rowing is a grand sport. Rowing a tender for a small cruising boat is a necessity. If you plan to tow or carry a dinghy at sea, it is as important to your convenience and independence to be able to operate it as it is to drive your automobile at home. When your cruising craft is at anchor or on a mooring, the dinghy serves as a jitney to transport provisions, ice, laundry, and crew members to and from shore. Although you may be a passenger much of the time, you should also learn to be the driver. Rowing lessons in a dinghy are best conducted under the same benign sea conditions as on the larger sister ship. Carry an experienced oarsman as a passenger until you can handle the craft skillfully enough to come alongside a dock or boat—an eggshell landing is true class. Learn and practice the correct knots for securing the dinghy to a boat or dock.

When you have confidence in your oarsmanship, try some solo trips in different weather conditions. Call on boating chums, fish for supper, visit the beach (remembering to leave the craft high enough to allow for a rising tide), or take a harbor tour in the sunset.

These preparatory steps should help to speed you through your shakedown. Don't be discouraged by the magnitude of the knowledge that is needed to be a pro in the boating field; much of the fun is in the learning. Heed the advice of the Water Rat in Kenneth Grahame's *The Wind in the Willows:* "Believe me, my young friend, there is *nothing,* absolutely nothing half so much worth doing as simply messing about in boats . . . In or out of 'em, it doesn't matter, that's the charm of it."

# 2. Layout and Accommodation

"Accomodation" is the Navy term for living and sleeping quarters on board a ship. It is more quaintly stated in another definition: "to hold without crowding." Keep this in mind the next time you clear the jeans and sweaters and hairbrushes from the cabin table to make room for the scrambled eggs and coffee, and then roll the sleepers out of their bunks to become the diners. An honest description of small boat cruising facilities is to spend a few days with good friends in a walk-in closet.

Small boat cabins are a compromise between space and comfort, and unless you design and build a craft for your specific needs, you must make the best possible use of an already existing plan. Many changes or additions that you may plan for your boating comfort are do-it-yourself projects; here is the place to apply your artistry

in woodworking and stitchery and to economize at the same time.

## Berths

The size and location of the dual-purpose berth/settees are important to cruising comfort. Most boat designs aim to provide space for as many sleeping bodies as possible; consequently, not every berth is fit for a king. Some are the invention of a jester, a discovery that we have made in the engineering exercise required for some dinette-to-sleeping berth conversions. You may not be able to change the design, but before you invite others to cruise on your boat, test each bunk yourself to know where to tuck that six-foot foredeck hand.

You *can* improve the comfort of your existing berths by providing top quality cushions (mattresses). The best cushion filling is synthetic foam, a firm, resilient, lightweight, fire- and water-resistant material well suited to boat living. The thickness of cushions over hard platforms should be a minimum of three inches for sleeping comfort.

Cushion cover materials must be able to take the rigors of life at sea. Coffee, gravy, peanuts, sunburn lotion and sea water will contribute to that "lived-in" look—best to use a fabric that can take it. You may have inherited a decorating scheme that is not your style at all, but if it doesn't give you nightmares, live with it long enough to look over the field. Inspect fit, color and fabric on cushions of other boats; seek competitive bids from boating firms and home decorators. Costs may vary as much as seventy-five percent, so it is worth your time and trouble. For real economy, if you are an experienced seamstress and own a stout sewing machine, make the covers yourself.

The choice of materials for cushion covers is important. Water-resistant vinyl is a practical covering on racing boats to survive the rough treatment of wet sails and foul weather gear brought down into the cabin to be "temporarily" stowed on the handiest bunk. It's practical on cruising boats in wet weather or when the cabin becomes a changing room for swimmers. The disadvantage of vinyl is the clinical appearance and slick surface, which readily slides pillows, sleeping bags, and sleepers off the berth in lumpy seas. Synthetic fabrics in textured weaves, tweeds, or plaids provide a warmer, home-like look and the texture helps to keep gear from slipping off to the cabin sole. Although not as tough as vinyl, these coverings will still withstand normal boat abuse.

You can have the best of both worlds by covering the bottom and back of each cushion in vinyl and using softer synthetic on the top, front, and sides. Turn the cushion over in wet weather or when in rigorous use to expose the more durable surface.

All cushion covers should be easily removable for washing, with rustproof closures running the length of the cushion; heavy plastic zipper tape and fittings bought from a sailmaker will outlast any covering. Welting at the seams gives a firmer fit and professional appearance. If you decide to change your color scheme, bring a *large* swatch of fabric aboard to be certain the dazzling pattern that looked so grand in the showroom doesn't overwhelm your small cabin.

## Pillows and Bedding

Sleeping pillows doubling as ornamental backrests should be the best quality that you can afford. Old rejects culled from home will collect dampness and mildew and will soon become quite unacceptable on board —far better to economize at sales in your local department store or to buy the better grade discount store models. Because down and feathers absorb moisture and lose resiliency in sea conditions, the best filling for boat pillows is Dacron polyester. Decorative covers should be generous enough to fit easily over the pillows. Choose a washable fabric with nonslip weave or texture, and if this is a home stitchery task, use your creativity to individualize each cover so that each crew member can identify his own pillow.

Sleeping bags or blankets? Or both? Because we try to extend the New England boating season from earliest May well into October, we use both. In spring and fall, for all northern waters, and for night passages, sleeping bags are our choice—there is something very comforting about tucking into that cozy primordial burrow when the wind and sea are only inches from your bunk. Envelope-style sleeping bags with synthetic filling and durable outer casings may be found in all marine and camping supply stores. Before you invest in sleeping bags for the crowd, try one in all temperature conditions; some outer fabric casings are so slippery that they slide off the berths, and are so tightly woven that the inside becomes a steam bath. For boat use, envelope-style bags are preferable to mummy models because they may be opened all the way to form a coverlet, may be zipped to a similar bag for a double, and spread out easily for airing or drying.

In warm climates, we use open weave acrylic blankets which, despite the more-boudoir-than-boat ribbon binding, are comfortable and practical for boat use, and also easily washable and fast-drying. Standard twin size blankets are generally too bulky for most narrow boat berths; cut a double bed blanket lengthwise, stitch up the cut edge, and you have two excellent berth coverings for just a little more than the cost of one. Woolen blankets may be divided in the same fashion. However, a disadvantage of wool is the constant shedding characteristic, which adds to the cleaning upkeep of the cabin sole.

Boat berths are rarely a perfect rectangle; consequently, fitting sheets is a challenge. The simplest solution is to use a twin flat (72″ × 96″ size) sheet, folded lengthwise, stitched across the bottom and 24 inches up the side. Cotton flannel sheets of this design are excellent for cold weather cruising. All fabrics should be easy-care cotton or polyester blend, and, to make it easy for each crew member to identify his own bedding, may be in different designs or colors.

## Bunkboards

If you plan to make long passages or night cruises on a sailboat, you should provide safety extensions to the inboard side of vulnerable berths for the protection of sleeping crew members. This device may be a board hinged at the outer edge of the bunk platform or a safety sling snapped to the platform and secured to the overhead; both are easily stowed under the bunk cushions when not in use.

## Port Covers

Some kind of curtain arrangement is necessary on cruising boats for cabin privacy alongside a dock or in a slip, and to keep the 4 A.M. sunrise from rousing the ship's company prematurely. Permanent curtain tracks are standard equipment on many modern boats; on a very small boat, a more spartan and less expensive substitute is a home-stitched port cover made of a simple rectangle of fabric, hemmed to fit the port and secured to the bulkhead with a small square of Velcro tape. These covers go up in a jiffy and stow easily under a bunk cushion. Sew the rough strip of the tape to the curtain and glue the *smooth* strip to the bulkhead to avoid dandy little sweater-catchers in the cabin.

## Screens

Flying insects are a nuisance on board a boat. The marauders invade your lovely protected harbor and gather for battle just as you settle back for the well-deserved sundowner. Be prepared with tight-fitting screens, which are readily available and can be installed in seconds. On small boats which have limited stowage space, you may make use of pliable plastic screens, edged in Velcro tape. These can be pressed into place against the overhead or bulkhead openings which are edged with the corresponding strips of *smooth* Velcro. For complete protection and proper ventilation in warm climates, you may need slides of screening material to guard the companionway.

## Decoration

Every lovely lady deserves a jewel or two—small paintings, photographs, wood carvings, macramé, or needle work adornments personalize your boat. Cover fragile paintings or photographs in laminated plastic for protection against water damage but *don't* cover needlepoint or similar works which retain moisture and attract mildew. Mount decorations well away from handrails and other safety fixtures. We have lived happily with Turk's-heads, cross-eyed tikis, wooden whales, and other cruising mementoes—may your boat's keepsakes bring you the same good luck on all your sea ventures.

## Lights

If you have ever plotted a course by flashlight in stormy sea conditions, held open the cover of an ice chest with one hand while you probed in the dark with the other, dropped a battery cap in the bilge, or brushed your teeth with shampoo, you will recognize the importance of proper lighting in work areas of a boat. The scattershot lighting arrangement of some boats may be improved by installing inexpensive supplementary fluorescent fixtures; these have the advantage of drawing little battery power for the luminosity they provide.

In planning the installation, position the lights carefully so that the beam doesn't interfere with the night vision of the helmsman. To conserve power and supplement cabin lighting, you may want to consider kerosene lamps. Marine supply stores and mail-order firms stock handsome replicas of antique lanterns which give a warm cozy light for dining or yarning with good friends at sea.

## Cabin Sole

The lovely teak and holly wood pattern on fine yachts of the past has given way to waffled fiberglass and carpeting. Fiberglass soles offer nonskid protection below but have a spartan appearance and require lots of elbow grease and a stout scrub brush to keep them clean. All-weather carpet is convenient on large power yachts, but on small craft is an un-nautical menace. The heeling angle of a sailing boat causes the carpet to slide and curl, resulting in an unsatisfactory and dangerous platform for anyone below deck. Carpet absorbs like a wick any water brought down into the cabin by sea boots, storm gear, bathing suits, deck hose, and sea spray, and feels clammy on every damp or foggy day thereafter.

## Lockers and Stowage

In this handy drawer, do you stow wrenches and pliers? Wallets and spectacles? Spoons and spatulas? Blocks and winch handles? Here is the true test of skipper/mate cooperation. You *both* must curb the pack rat instinct and bring aboard your boat only the gear that you really need. Sometimes what I really need is ten pounds of chocolate but I know that I have to leave some other treasure at home to make room for my addiction. Early established patterns of stowing will cling, so unless you are solo cruising, don't fill every available locker with your possessions or you will usurp the space needed by guests and crew when they join the boat. Keep it simple. That handy-dandy little egg poacher that lives four layers down in the pot locker may *never* see an egg.

## Ventilation

Any accumulation of odors from the engine, galley or smokers can pollute a small boat cabin enough to turn a slightly queasy sailor into a seasick invalid. To provide proper ventilation, it is necessary to allow clear passage of air *in* and *out* of the boat, usually *in* the companionway and *out* the forward hatch. Both are also entries for unwanted rain or sea water, particularly the forward hatch under way. Dorade ventilators in strategic areas such as the galley and head allow air intake without moisture and may be turned to face the wind direction when the boat is in a slip or at a dock.

In tropical climates or in summer heat, a windscoop rigged at the forward hatch directs constant air into the cabin. Ordered from a sailmaker or made at home with a heavy duty sewing machine, the scoop will add immeasurably to the comfort in the cabin on hot airless days and nights.

## Head

On small wooden cruising boats of the past, an enclosed head was a luxury. Today's fiberglass construction makes possible a separate compartment for the toilet and basin, and sometimes additional locker space. For the convenience of all boat members, you should supply a mirror, properly mounted and lighted for shaving; rods or hooks for towels and washcloths; soap container; toilet paper holder; and a small wastebasket securely mounted for sea. So that the communal cup doesn't spread a communal cold, provide small disposable paper cups. Other necessities are spare toilet paper, soap, and paper tissues, the latter item to be discarded in the wastebasket, *not* in the toilet. Post clear directions for the use of the marine toilet to supplement your instructions.

In any dry locker space, "dry" is theoretical, and it is wise to wrap supplies of bed and bath linen in labelled plastic bags. Additional locker space may be used for toilet kits belonging to you and your guests, a waterproof box of health aids and common pharmaceuticals, cleaning supplies, and toilet brush. Reserve space for boat emergency medical supplies, which should be stored in a waterproof container. These are for use in real medical emergencies, not the least splinter; this will be discussed further in Chapter 9 on first aid. An inventory of useful health and pharmaceutical aids appears in the back of the book in Appendix C.

Unlike the customary counsel that "nothing is too good for the boat," towels and washcloths may be second rate. Thick luxurious models fill precious locker space, take forever to dry at shore laundromats, and, once wet aboard, *never* dry. Cheap cotton/synthetic towels of 21" × 36" dimensions are generous enough for use on board, adequate for showers ashore, and won't cause you anguish if they are left behind at the last marina. You may solve the identification problem by providing different colors or designs for each crew member. Swimming towels in standard 26" × 46" dimensions may need to be shared on extended cruises— the more extensive the cruise, the more the sharing of *everything* becomes routine.

# Cockpit

The cockpit of a small boat leads a double life. During racing or rigorous passagemaking conditions, for the convenience and safety of the helmsman and crew members working the boat, it must be free of clutter. At dockings and in sail changes, books or hats or spectacles can be swept overboard with the spaghetti of lines—stow cushions and other treasures in the cabin during these maneuvers.

On serene passages and at anchor, the cockpit is your verandah. For comfort and good looks, some boats are equipped with custom deck cushions, a blessing on a lovely day, but a liability in rough or wet weather, when cushions may become sodden under the casing or be blown overboard. Consider well the extra care and stowage space which these fineries require before making an expensive investment. Inexpensive U.S. Coast Guard-approved life cushions, available in a variety of colors, may be an adequate substitute.

After your long hours of planning and shopping comes the reward—a well-equipped snug home at sea. In *Spring Tides,* Samuel Eliot Morison describes it well: "Possibly this love for a small cabin was atavistic, derived from our ancestors for whom a small cave was the only safe, indeed the only possible dwelling. Whatever the origin, it was part of a yearning for something compact, small, closed-in from the world." This is the place for the long after-breakfast coffees and evening sundowners and the music and good books and the gam with good friends at sea.

# 3. The Galley

Like the hearth of Colonial times, the galley of a small boat is the center of all activity. Your kitchen is the main corridor, conversation hall, sail bin, and changing room; for sharing this multi-purpose territory, you will need the agility of an acrobat and the disposition of an angel. But you will never be lonely, nor will you lack for attentive scullery help. Enjoy the center of the circle role and learn to turn out superlative meals in your child's playhouse.

## Stoves

A well-designed efficient stove is a vital piece of equipment on a boat where a rocking platform, gusty air currents and occasional moisture accompany the cook-

ing procedure. You need all the help you can get with the best model possible. The size of your boat and the space allowance of the galley will dictate your choice of galley stove, as will the extent of your cruising. For day sailing and short overnights when you will prepare basic meals and reheat previously prepared dishes, a simple two-burner stove is probably adequate; for longer cruising and racing, a gimballed stove is essential for safe meal preparation; live-aboard cruising and cooking for a crowd will be easier if you use a gimballed three-burner stove with oven. But before you decide to trade in an existing stove, clean it and replace any faulty parts—it may turn out to be a trusty friend, and will save you an investment in an unknown model. Consult the list below to determine the model best suited to you.

### TWO-BURNER NONGIMBALLED STOVE

Advantages:
> Takes little space.
> Efficient fuel consumption.

Disadvantages:
> Difficult and unsafe in heeling position of sailboat.
> Baking, roasting, casserole heating limited to "camp style" top-of-stove or Dutch oven cooking.

### TWO-BURNER GIMBALLED STOVE

Advantages:
> Takes only a little more space than nongimballed model.
> Cooking in heeling sailboat is possible.
> Efficient fuel consumption.

Disadvantages:
> Baking, roasting, casserole heating limited to "camp style" top-of-stove or Dutch oven cooking.

THREE-BURNER GIMBALLED STOVE WITH OVEN

Advantages:

Generous stove-top surface for holding food before serving.

Bakes, roasts, heats pre-cooked or frozen dishes as in home oven.

Crisps or dries crackers, cereals, etc.

Oven heats cabin in cold weather.

When not in use, oven provides safe stowage for perishable foods, e.g., cakes, breads, cookies.

Disadvantages:

Stove takes up large space in galley.

Oven uses large amount of fuel.

Oven overheats cabin in hot weather.


SEA-SWING STOVE

Advantages:

Safest method of cooking in rough seas.

Provides a supplementary burner to meal preparation.

Disadvantages:

Limits cooking to one pan or double boiler.

Slow cooking if using canned heat (Sterno).


# Fuels

In the past, traditional stove fuels were coal, kerosene, and alcohol, available in most ports for a modest sum. Today, coal is seldom used on pleasure yachts in this country (with the exception of extreme northern latitudes). Alcohol is probably the most popular fuel, kerosene less so. Bottled gas is becoming increasingly popular with modern boat construction that permits safe stowage of gas containers. Listed briefly below are the characteristics of these modern fuels.

## ALCOHOL

Advantages:
  Clean flame.
  Primes with same fuel.
  Flame easily extinguished with water.
  Safest of fuels listed.
Disadvantages:
  Fuel is expensive.
  Priming operation requires time.
  Least efficient cooking fuel.

## KEROSENE

Advantages:
  Inexpensive and readily available fuel.
Disadvantages:
  Unpleasant odor in less than perfect conditions.
  Smoky flame causes soot in cabin.
  Moderately efficient cooking fuel.
  Requires other fuel for priming.

## BUTANE, PROPANE

Advantages:
  Clean flame.
  Instant cooking without priming.
  Most efficient cooking fuel.
Disadvantages:
  Explosive fuel.
  Requires well-maintained safety shut-offs.
  Fuel facilities not universally available.

## CANNED HEAT

Canned heat (Sterno) is a supplementary cooking fuel, and therefore is not to be compared with other regular fuels. In rough seas and heavy weather conditions, this fuel is invaluable—the high cost and slow burning characteristic are small penalties to pay for the safety feature of a small containable fuel used in a gimballed Sea-Swing stove.

## Auxiliary Cooking Methods

Popular on many boats is a charcoal grill designed to fit into the flagstaff socket at the stern of the boat; it is a welcome method of relieving the cook, giving the outdoor chef a chance to shine, and keeping the cabin cool below. Use it in fine weather when it isn't blowing a gale. If you invest in this appliance, take these precautions: avoid overzealous priming, keep the flames under control with a ready water container, don't leave the fire unattended, and watch for sudden wind shifts which might send flames back in the boat. Any open fire aboard a boat, especially a gasoline-powered one, is a potential hazard and should be treated as such; a sudden flare-up can not only ruin a meal in seconds, but can cause serious damage to your boat.

To guard against burns, the cook should use long-handled implements and protective gloves. When not in use, the grill may be wrapped in a stout canvas bag to protect other boat gear; stow *well away* from the compass to prevent deviation in that instrument.

## Ice Chest

The most convenient ice chest is not necessarily the largest. The most efficient models are well-insulated, are top-loading with a lid which may be secured in the open position, have a screened drain to prevent clogging of the outlet hose, and are no deeper than the reach of the cook. Some Bermuda racing boats, equipped to store heartening steaks for their crews of nine, sport icy caverns that require a headstand by the cook to capture each meal—this type of hunting is not recommended on a small boat in a seaway. An oversized sea chest is a rarity but if you are blessed with such a treasure, build a partition within the chest to isolate food supplies and ice when provisions are low.

## Sink

The galley sink serves dual purposes. The first, and obvious one, is as a place to wash dishes and prepare food; the second, as a safe haven in all sea conditions for the teakettle, hot pans, and cups and glasses during meal preparation. It should be deep enough to hold these safely. Don't be surprised at the other treasures which find their way there in emergencies—winch handles, spectacles, gloves, caps, beer cans, shells, wildflowers, and live lobsters. Generosity in size is not always a virtue; beware the large shallow sink that looks grand until the boat's motion creates a wave system *inside* the sink—up and over the edge with every roll of the ship. When your supply of fresh water is limited, you can't afford to fill it anyway.

## Water Conservation

Many modern boats are equipped with a pressure water system, often providing hot water after the use of the engine—very convenient for cruising comfort, but a luxury that can be misused. We are home-conditioned to wash, brush teeth, shave, and rinse everything under a stream of water from the faucet, habits which are hard to lose at sea. Inexperienced crew members and careless mariners can quickly deplete the fresh water supply of a boat and may need to be reminded about restraint and economy when using a boat pressure system. The alternative is to squander your precious cruising time in port to fill the tanks.

Hand pumps, requiring human effort for each drop of water, provide a brake on water supply; this manual system draws no power from the boat battery, is certainly quieter, and may cut your water consumption in half. You will need at least one hand pump if you plan long offshore trips. For very long passages at sea and in areas which have limited water supplies, you will be well advised to install a salt water pump at the galley sink; this supplementary supply is fine for washing galleyware (rinsing knives and other cutlery in fresh water to inhibit rusting), and in small amounts may be added to fresh water for cooking.

Careful dishwashing procedures will conserve the fresh water supply. A system that was successful for us during a dry winter season in the Caribbean, where rum flows like a mountain stream and water runs like lava, was ludicrous but effective. All galley utensils were washed and rinsed in two 5½″ × 8″ plastic food containers which fitted side by side in the sink. With this arrangement, we could clean all except the large pans in a few jiggers of water.

## Garbage Disposal

We are crowding our land and ocean with waste. In a small boat, it is shocking to watch the accumulation of so much trash for so few people—it's out of all proportion to the size of the craft. Somehow we must find an ecological compromise that preserves the beauty of the sea, and yet keeps the boat from becoming a garbage scow.

On short trips with frequent shore stops, all waste may be collected in heavy plastic bags and stored in the towed dinghy or on the afterdeck (secure well to keep from losing it), and disposed ashore without sullying the sea. On longer cruises in offshore waters where this is impossible, you must separate and compact all trash for disposal at sea. Unless you are crossing the ocean, some waste must still be reserved for shore disposal.

The following items may be discarded at sea:

> Glass containers—fill with sea water to prevent floating.

Metal cans—pierce or open at top and bottom to prevent floating.

Untreated paper products and boxes.

Galley waste from meat, shellfish, vegetables, fruit —cut melon and citrus rinds into small pieces.

These items should not be discarded at sea:

Plastic bottles and containers.

Styrofoam cups and egg cartons.

Treated and waxed dairy containers.

Plastic bags.

*Never* throw waste of any kind into harbor waters or near land where it may be washed ashore.

## Counters

The yards of Formica in a home kitchen will seem scandalously wasteful after you have worked in a boat galley. Efficiently arranged and kept absolutely free of clutter, the doily-sized counter area in a small boat will serve you well. An additional wood surface for cutting, preferably large enough to prepare sandwiches, is useful; some boats are fitted with a stove-top cutting board that slides out of the way when the stove is used for cooking. Fiddles or protective lips at the inboard side help to keep food and utensils in place.

## Lockers

There is *never* enough stowage space in a small boat. You can double the efficiency of the locker area, however, with careful planning, a measuring tape, and the assistance of a cooperative carpenter. Before you cut and drill and glue shelves and fixtures, spend a few cruising days to determine the best use of your galley space, and if you have time, make a template or mockup plan of custom-designed glass and cup racks, cutlery drawers and other space savers. Several narrow shelves may be better than one large one; dividers keep food and dishes securely separated in rough seas; lipped shelves and shock cords hold food supplies in place in a heeling sailboat. All frequently used staples, condiments, and utensils should be easily reachable by the cook working in a safety harness. Be an architect for a day and have the best galley your boat can provide.

## Safety in the Galley

Recognizing that most household accidents occur in the kitchen and adding the hazard of a moving platform make obvious the need for proper safety gear in a boat galley. All utensils, especially heavy or sharp tools, should be permanently stowed; knives and sharp implements should be protected. A gimballed stove should be guarded with a bar to prevent cook and crew from being thrown against it in heavy weather.

A safety harness is essential to the safety of the cook tending the galley in rough weather; this safety strap, or "tailgate," is usually made of stout webbing or sailstop material, fits behind the buttocks, and is secured with snaphooks at either end to eyebolts. To determine the design which will provide you with good leaning support and enough mobility at the stove and sink, have two crew members to hold a line behind you at hip level—*your* hip level, not that of the basketball player foredeck hand—while the boat is heeling.

Barefoot freedom may be part of boat living, but in the galley, spills of hot liquid and flying utensils can turn you into a case study for orthopedic surgery. If you value your feet, wear shoes in the galley.

## Fire Protection

Keep the area around and over the stove clear of inflammable articles such as curtains, dish towels, and paper goods—particularly paper towels, which often unwind in a breezy boat cabin. For your safety, before lighting the stove remove anything you will need from any lockers in back of the stove. Keep a currently inspected fire extinguisher nearby, and, most important of all, establish a safe routine for the operation of the stove by *everyone*.

Before priming alcohol stoves, partially fill a teakettle with water to have a readily available supply in the event of a sudden flare-up. Alcohol fires from defective fuel, improper priming, or stove malfunction generally look more menacing than they are and may be extinguished quickly with a small amount of water.

When using butane or propane stoves, turn off safety valves when the stove is not in use.

## Galley Fire

A blaze or fire in an alcohol stove may be extinguished with water, salt, or baking soda. The flames generally reduce themselves quickly, but if they persist, *sprinkle* with water or smother with a damp cloth or dish towel. Use a fire extinguisher if the fire is out of control and could spread to other areas of the boat. Guard against fuel which may spill on your clothing.

Do *not* pour water on a kerosene blaze. Smother with a damp cloth or towel, or use a fire extinguisher.

A fire or an explosion of escaping gas from butane or propane is an immediate hazard. Use a fire extinguisher at once and have all crew members leave the dangerous area. When the fire is under control, turn off all burner and safety valves. With judicious practice of safety rules, you should never have to use these instructions at all.

# 4. Clothing, Personal Gear and Grooming

## Clothing

What to wear? Will you need a grand new wardrobe for this boating life? And will you look like all those handsome advertisements—slick hair, shining shoes and knife-press slacks? If you do, you'll be the only one in the fleet—and a great embarassment to your skipper. For most of your time aboard, the same comfortable jeans, workshirts, and pullovers that you wear for window-washing or gardening at home will be appropriate. The traditional U.S. Navy garb of dungarees, work shirt, stout deck shoes, and watch cap is just as practical today as it was a hundred years ago and it will be your standby.

Very important to your comfort on board is proper

footwear and foul weather gear. Fine storm jackets, storm trousers, and deck shoes are expensive, but should last for years with normal use. Before you make the investment, ask knowledgeable boating friends for their recommendations, and compare the price and quality of the different varieties. Deck shoes should be large enough to fit over socks. Foul weather gear should slip easily over layers of heavy sweaters and slacks without the bound-up "mummy" look. Bib-overall storm trousers are important to the crew members tending the foredeck, but not essential for cockpit duties, and for a woman, very inconvenient for trips to the head.

## Shore Clothes

Most social occasions in the course of a cruise require nothing more formal than clean slacks and shirts for men and women. Deck shoes or boat sandals are best for maneuvering in and out of the dinghy and onto slippery docks and ladders. Some clubs and restaurants require jacket and tie for men, but again, the footwear should be practical. Small boats have limited locker space, so leave long overcoats and raincoats at home and be economical about your wardrobe—there just isn't the time, space, or privacy for a fashion show on board.

## Recommended Clothing for 10 Days of Cruising—Moderate Climate

1 suit of foul weather gear—top with hood or sou'-wester and pants.
2 pairs long pants—slacks or jeans.
2 pairs shorts—or culottes for women.
5 short-sleeved shirts.
1 long-sleeved shirt.
1 bathing suit—fast-drying, *not* cut-offs.

1 night garment—long T-shirts make fine boat night-wear.

1 heavy wool sweater.

1 shore-going sweater.

1 cap with sun-protecting brim—if straw, foldable.

Fast-drying underwear.

Socks.

1 set slacks and jacket or slacks and top for dinners ashore.

1 shore-going skirt for women—reversible wrapa-rounds for variety with a pin to secure the flip side when you are boarding or leaving docks and din-ghies.

Scarves—for women.

1 pair of deck shoes.

1 pair of other shoes—sneakers or sandals.

## Optional Clothing for Moderate Climate

Sea boots.

Windbreaker or jacket—presentable enough to wear ashore in the evening.

Windshirt—light nylon shell of the sort worn by ski-ers.

## Recommended Clothing for 10 Days of Cruising—Hot Climate

1 light-weight foul weather top with hood or sou'-wester—trousers if night passages or long watches are planned.

1 pair long pants—slacks or jeans, cotton preferable.

3 pairs shorts—jogging shorts, cotton preferable.

5 short-sleeved shirts, cotton preferable.

2 long-sleeved shirts—for sun protection.

2 bathing suits.

1 light night garment.

1 medium-weight sweater.

2 caps with sun-protecting brims.

Fast-drying underwear.

1 set slacks and jacket, or slacks and top, for dinners ashore.

1 pair of deck shoes.

1 pair of sandals or canvas shoes—for reefs and beach.

## Optional Clothing for Hot Climate

1 light-weight sweater or shawl for women.

1 long cotton skirt or caftan for women.

1 long-sleeved shirt and one pair pants—to wear swimming for protection from the sun.

1 pair socks—for protection from the sun.

## Recommended Clothing for 10 Days of Cruising—Cold Climate

1 suit of foul weather gear—top with hood or sou'-wester and pants.

3 pairs long pants—1 pair heavy cloth or wool.

5 long-sleeved shirts—2 cotton knit turtleneck or equivalent.

1 bathing suit.

1 warm night garment.

2 heavy wool sweaters.

1 long-sleeved wool or cotton flannel shirt.

1 wool cap or watch cap.

Fast-drying underwear.

Long johns.

5 pairs of warm socks.

1 pair deck shoes.

1 pair sea boots.

1 pair of extra-heavy socks to wear under sea boots.

Gloves or mittens.

1 pair of waterproof rubber gloves—of the type worn

by lobstermen—for use in handling wet lines and
deck gear.

Scarf, small terrycloth towel, or other neckwear—to
wear under foul weather top for protection from
rain.

1 warm jacket or ski-type parka.

## Optional Clothing for Cold Climate

Warm-up track pants—wear over slacks on night
watch.

Vest with down or fiber filling—of the type worn by
campers.

## Jewelry

A short tip about wearing fine jewelry on board small
cruising boats: *don't.* It is easy to shatter or lose rings,
watches, or pendants in the commotion of deck maneuvers or swimming. When you wear your holiday best
or "dress for dinner," pop on some dime store treasures.
No one will question Tiffany vs. Woolworth, and you
will be free from worry.

## Clothes Lockers

Although clothes stowage is generally located in a dry
part of the boat, moisture sometimes creeps in unin-
vited. If you are in doubt about the condition of the
clothes locker areas on your boat, it is wise to use protective plastic bags. Check the space assigned to the crew,
too. We were amused by the empty garbage bags
brought on board by a cruising friend of long standing
until we discovered that his locker had *always* leaked.
Shore clothes should be covered with a plastic garment
bag and hung on rustproof hangers marked in some way
to identify the clothes of each crew member.

## Cleanliness and Grooming

Sea life is not synonymous with personal neglect. The old adage, "Time to bathe is when you smell a horse on board" is for the lubberly. If the temperature of the water is warm enough for swimming, it is probably fine for a wash and shampoo at the swimming ladder. Using a bath sponge and the same detergent that you use for dishwashing, you can easily remove the patina of salt, sweat, and sunburn cream; towel off immediately to avoid salt buildup on your hair and skin.

In colder waters, unless you have polar bear lineage, you must resort to the "little bird bath" technique in the head, but check the fresh water supply and the schedule of other boat members before you tie up the head for any length of time.

Scheduling time for morning use of the head is a challenge. For most of us, the least flexible part of the day is the morning cleanup, but unfortunately, facilities in a small boat don't allow time for everyone to follow his favorite schedule. Generally, everyone on board wakes to a common cock's crow, which means that each crew member is ready to use the washing, toothbrushing, hair-combing, shaving and toilet facilities at the same moment. Four or five crew members become a cast of thousands. A capable cruising friend and valued foredeck hand eases his 220-pound frame into the small head of a boat and emerges five minutes later, slick and shaved and shining—ready to cook omelets for the crowd. Most of us, however, are less adroit and must postpone our lengthy ablutions until later in the day. When you are breakfast cook, use the "lick and a promise" grooming technique when you first arise—the captain and crew will sing hallelujahs over your pancakes but will never notice your hairdo.

You and your boatmates will need the same pharmaceuticals and health aids on board that you use at home. Keep a waterproof box of these items*available to all, but do *not* confuse it with the boat's medical first aid kit. Consult a checklist of all toilet articles and sundries that you may need for your cruise—thirty miles off the coast is not the time to run out of your favorite roll-on or sunscreen. One beauty aid that is best left at home is hair spray. A boat cabin is just too small for the permeating odor and possible damage to wood surfaces of the boat.

Every sailor carries a ditty bag containing tape, needles and thread, and other small articles for repairs at sea. Be sure that you have all the necessary supplies for quick stitchery on board.

---

*A recommended list of health and pharmaceutical aids for cruising appears in Appendix C.

# 5. Preparation for the Cruise

## The Notebook

Unless you have the memory of a computer, you will need a boat reminder; mine is a pocket-sized 4″ × 7″ looseleaf notebook. It is my filing cabinet, my conscience, and the source of this information:

Inventory and stowage location of galley staples, paper goods, cleaning supplies, drugs and pharmeuticals, stove fuel, lamp oil, liquor, beer, boat linen, galley gear list.

List of personal clothing for all climates.

Commissioning and decommissioning checklist.

Port facilities—updated list of fuel, water, ice, groceries, liquor supplies; post office, laundromat, hardware store, restaurant, taxis in each harbor.

Names of boats and owners met on cruising holidays.
Crew list—names, addresses and phone numbers of
cruising chums; also, to prod an unreliable memory:
food preferences, special diets, excellence (or defi-
ciency) of hearing, sight, helmsmanship of friends
and crew members—all of which will help us keep
the nearsighted pals off the fog watch, the seasick
out of the rolling galley, and the beer in proper supply.

## Pre-cruise Tasks

An empty boat is easier to clean than one that is fully
stocked. Before bringing aboard provisions for a cruise,
give the ice chest and food and pot lockers a scrub; clean
and check clothes storage areas for possible leaks; brush
and clean under bunk cushions to remove cookie
crumbs, peanuts, and other mementoes of earlier passages; clean the head and cabin sole. Now you are ready
to stow.

## Food Stowage

Stocking a boat for a long cruise or holiday or even for
a weekend is easy if you can cadge help in handing
supplies aboard and down the companionway. Sturdy
ice bags are a lifesaver for toting gear and supplies because they fold flat and stow easily for re-supplying or
off-loading. The cheap and handy grocery carton is best
unloaded from the cockpit, or, in tropic areas, from the
dock or dinghy to avoid infestation by cockroaches and
other critters who dwell in the cardboard recesses and
are enchanted by the seagoing haven of dark lockers on
a boat. These unwelcome tenants multiply fast and are
hard to evict.

Establish a pattern for orderly food stowage and stick
with it to help you find supplies when the going is rough
—rolling food cans on the cabin sole make the job of pin

boy in a bowling alley look enviable. Limitations of iced storage and locker space on a boat often make it necessary to adopt different methods from home storage for keeping supplies fresh and safe. Below are a few tricks of the trade.

## CANNED GOODS

Buy first-quality provisions—there is no room for second-rate food products on a boat.

Identify the contents on the top of the tin with a waterproof marker. This prevents gastronomic chaos should the labels wash off in damp lockers.

Food in dented or rusty cans is safe when there are no leaks or bulges—use these cans before undamaged goods. Food in bulged or leaking cans is *unsafe* and should be discarded.

## DRY STAPLES

Cereals, flour, rice, sugar, tea—store in labelled waterproof containers with tight-fitting lids.

Mixes—remove inner food packets from cardboard boxes (which may disintegrate in damp lockers), cut out label and cooking directions and store together in sealed plastic bags.*

Cookies, crackers, snacks—after opening, store in well-sealed plastic containers*(but who ever heard of leftover cookies?).

## DAIRY PRODUCTS

In cool climates, the products discussed below will keep for weeks without ice if stored in a low locker near or below the waterline:

Cheese—hard or wax-covered varieties such as Ched-

*These precautions may not be necessary for short cruises.

dar, Edam, Havarti, Swiss, unopened soft processed cheeses such as American, Gruyère.

Margarine (not soft variety).

Long-life milk (available in some tropic areas).

Eggs (buy the best quality available).

These products must be stored on ice:

Butter—remove from wrapping and store in plastic box with lid.

Cheese—soft perishable varieties such as cottage, cream, blue, Roquefort. Be wary of strong-smelling cheese. In the unreliable temperatures of an ice chest these can be overassertive to vile.

Soft margarine—this is not an economical product for its bulk, especially in limited ice chest space.

Fresh milk—store close to ice in deep plastic containers. Tipping or leaking of milk cartons can sour the entire ice chest. Unopened cartons should remain fresh for a week.

Sour cream, yogurt—place containers in plastic bin next to ice.

### FISH, MEAT, AND POULTRY

In cool climates and cold waters, these items will keep for weeks in low lockers or stored below the waterline:

Canned meats.

Corned beef.

Smoked meats—ham, slab bacon.

Pepperoni and some hard sausages.

These perishables should be stored in the coldest part of the ice chest:

Fresh beef, fish, lamb, poultry, pork, sausage, sliced bacon, veal, cold cuts—do *not* remove vacuum-sealed wrappings, but *do* remove butcher's paper.

Seal in *heavy* aluminum foil, label, and store in plastic bag or container. It is best to keep meats from direct contact with ice; this causes juices to bleed, leaving the meat edible but unappetizingly gray. In planning menus, use the most perishable products first, such as poultry, fish, and pork. Your nose will tell you when it is "passing"—you can often salvage the center part of beef or lamb cuts by scraping away and discarding the outside layer and cooking the remainder immediately. Do *not* salvage questionable fish, poultry, or pork products.

A word of caution concerning the preparation of fresh chicken: contaminating bacteria can adhere to knives, cutting boards and skin that has come into contact with uncooked poultry. Wash hands and implements well after handling.

## FRUIT

Fresh fruit is a popular treat aboard a boat, but requires a little tender loving care to keep it from being damaged in sea conditions and also to keep everything from ripening at once. Most fruit keeps well unwashed and stored in the open air.

Apples—excellent keeping qualities.

Bananas—buy some partially ripe and some green for later in the cruise.

Citrus fruits—excellent keeping qualities.

Apricots, cherries, grapes, peaches, pears—separate pieces of these fragile fruits with layers of paper towelling.

Berries—highly perishable; must be eaten immediately.

Melons—store in cool part of boat for even ripening.

Dried fruits—apricots, dates, prunes and raisins are good snacks after fresh fruit is gone, and therapeutic for those suffering from constipation.

## VEGETABLES

Many vegetables which we refrigerate at home will keep well in a well-ventilated, cool part of a boat. Store in net bags or bins; plastic bags will cause rotting.

These products keep well in cool dry storage:

Acorn squash, beets, carrots, cabbages, garlic, onions, parsnips, potatoes, shallots, turnips.

These vegetables are more perishable, but if not over-ripe when purchased will keep in a well-ventilated part of the boat:

Cucumbers, eggplants, peppers, tomatoes, zucchini.

Perishable products which should go on ice are:

Asparagus, beans, broccoli, cauliflower, celery, peas, scallions.

Lettuce—remove outer leaves, wrap loosely in foil and wash only when ready to use.

Parsley—wash well and store upright in water in covered plastic container.

Radishes—wash and remove leaves.

Mint, fresh herbs—store in plastic bags and wash only when ready to use.

## BREAD AND BAKERY PRODUCTS

Bread—double-wrapped unsliced bread stays fresh and resists mold. Hearty dark breads such as pumpernickel keep best.

Fruit breads—banana, date, and apple breads are versatile but must be watched carefully for mold.

Brownies, fruit cakes, date and fruit bars—these keep well in damp sea conditions (but if you can keep them for long, you are indeed a miser).

Frozen cakes and coffee cakes—when stored in the ice chest will keep for a week.

Warning: Cream pies and desserts with cream fillings should not be kept on a boat without refrigeration;

the temperature inside an ice chest is not sufficiently cold to prevent the growth of bacteria which can cause food poisoning.

A list of suggested food staples is in Appendix B.

## Efficient Use of an Ice Chest

A warm ice chest absorbs a great quantity of ice before reaching a temperature satisfactory for keeping perishables—buy enough to allow for this shrinkage. Block ice lasts longer than cubes. In some remote areas where block ice is not available, it may be possible to obtain flake ice from a fish plant or cannery; sometimes there is no charge, and *you* supply the large-size garbage bags and labor. Unclean water source and handling conditions may make chipped ice unsafe in beverages. In some cruising areas, there is *no* ice; as you restock your larder from the local store, investigate the possibility of placing a small plastic container in someone's freezer overnight for a fee. We have been the lucky recipients of this hospitality in remote Newfoundland ports, where the residents would accept no payment, but were delighted to share a "mug up" with us on our boat.

To preserve your ice supply on a cruise, cut down on constant opening of the ice chest by removing at one time all perishables required for a meal; chop a large chunk of ice to be chipped into drink-size bits in an ice bucket later. Buy cold beer and soda to go directly on ice; to forestall grand upheavals of the contents of the ice chest by the thirsty crew, stow cold drinks in a readily accessible part. Wrap all produce and meat carefully to prevent paper or food particles from clogging the drain. If you have planned judiciously, you will find that your fresh food supply has given out with the ice—time to scrub the ice chest and switch to cans, or sail into port for restocking.

# Float Plan

Preparations for receiving messages and mail while you are cruising should be made in advance. Yacht clubs and marinas are logical choices for holding mail and messages, but in a short and hectic season, in spite of the good intentions of the staff, your communiqués may be lost in the shuffle. Post offices in the towns you intend to visit will hold mail addressed to General Delivery; however, this means a firm commitment on your part to enter that port. The best courier is your arriving crew.

In unfamiliar towns, there is always a police station or sheriff's office and everyone in town knows the location; the officers are cooperative about receiving messages of *important,* although perhaps not emergency, nature. Please be a courteous and thoughtful mariner—do not misuse this service.

To provide finances for your cruise, carry traveler's checks or cash to cover expenses along the way—bring more money than you think you will need. Prices of food and other supplies which are easily reached from boat harbors are often higher than in your home supermarket. Some banks and specialty markets which cater to the tourist trade will accept a personal check, but don't count on it.

Careful planning and credit cards don't cover every unforeseen expense. Should there be a medical emergency or extensive malfunction of the boat, you may need cash—and fast. In rare situations, after prearrangement with my bank officer at home, I have asked the bank manager of the town in which we were stranded to call my home bank, describe my appearance (if you change your hair color, your banker should be first to know), and verify the bank balance to cover the amount of my personal check.

# Crew Briefing

Before leaving home, give your guests and crew members a float plan with your estimated schedule, message center in the event of unexpected delays, and an accurate description of your meeting place. For late arrivals who may not be familiar with your boat, provide specific information about the color and size of the yacht and the flags you will be flying. This will avoid long and needless searches by exhausted crew members, who may end up creeping aboard at midnight after two hours of touring the harbor in search of a white sloop you neglected to mention had been painted blue.

Share with the crew your intentions for passagemaking, laundry stops and shore meals so that they may pack and budget accordingly. On small boats, there is no stowage space for hard suitcases; advise the guests to carry soft duffels (laundry bags will do). Obtain from your late arriving crew a dependable phone number, preferably at business, should you need to call along the way—standing in the rain in a public phone booth waiting out teenage telephonitis is not a fun way to spend a holiday. Most chums ask what they may contribute for the trip. Tell them and you won't be surprised with unnecessary unstowables.

# 6. Comfort and Contentment of the Crew

Like the wandering albatross, some mariners roam the seas in independent solitude, but most of us are gulls and petrels, needing and seeking the companionship of other sea birds. For us is the camaraderie of small boat living, often lacking in the business lunch/cocktail circuit ashore. We generally choose old cruising chums for shipmates; life is easy because everyone fits instantly into a harmonious boat routine. But cruising can be fun with neophytes too; it is invigorating to introduce boating to newcomers. In this case, ease gently into extended cruising by trying an overnight or weekend trip together first. Small boat life is not for everyone; sharing basic accommodations in close quarters, lack of privacy, and seasickness are just a few factors which can bring misery even to an experienced mariner, and two weeks later at sea is not the time to find this out.

# Welcoming the Crew

Although you have had the responsibility of organizing the cruise and outfitting the boat, your guests and crew have also been busy with house-closings, baby sitters, job assignments, transportation plans, last minute details and other chores to keep them up half the night before the trip. They will be excited and exhausted, so welcome them with open arms, time for a swim, change from shore clothing, a cool drink—not necessarily in that order. Their nesting instinct is strong; show them the location of their lockers and berths, and postpone your harbor departure, if you can, until they have stowed their gear and changed to boat clothes.

The ideal time for crew arrival is late afternoon, in time for a swim, sundowner, festive dinner and good night's sleep. However, since time and tide wait for no man, mate, or honored guest, your schedule may require instant sailing; if so, take it easy on deck tasks for your crew until they are acclimated to the boat. We once introduced a Chesapeake Bay-to-New York Harbor passage to contemporary newlyweds in this fashion: speedy supper in foul weather gear; port departure in black of night, fresh winds, sprightly seas; drill for setting new twin jibs, lifting poles *and* mate several feet above the foredeck; incapacitating the cruising chum; scaring the daylights out of his bride; shorthanding and shorttempering the skipper. Happily, the next morning found us all soaring along the Jersey Coast at hull speed and still friends, but with kinder foresight on our part, we could have had a less exhilarating start.

Seasoned sailors adapt readily to life on board and need only a short briefing on the charted course and the location of boat safety gear. Novices are eager to learn but are easily confused by an immediate diet of indigestible sea lore. Curb your mother hen instincts and dole out tasks and explanations slowly to enable the newcomer to develop one skill at a time. There is a useful job for *everyone* on board; you will soon find the best use of the talents of the new recruit. An erratic helmsman may be a creative cook, a nearsighted crew member may be a powerful winch-grinder, and the delicate lass may be a dandy buoy-spotter. If everyone can "play," your cruise will be a success.

## Morale

Until they have shipboard experience, junior Naval officers are assigned the hypothetical tasks of laundry and morale—cartoon ignominy. On your small boat, the job may be yours, and it's no laughing matter. The mood of the sea can change abruptly from arctic cold to tropic heat, and from hurricane to glassy calm. Days of these extremes give some people cabin fever—claustrophobia with a touch of misanthropy. Recognize the symptoms and treat the malady before it spreads. It often helps to shake up the bag a bit. If you have been cruising long days without respite and the routine has become burdensome, take a day of shore leave; a beach picnic with wine and siesta; rendezvous with another boat for a gam, awards at dinner, chocolate bars and mints; celebrate birthdays, holidays or National Foot Health Week. Celebrate *anything*. If everyone is bored with sedate passages and you have enough experienced watchstanders, plan a night sail in fine weather.

The old Nova Scotian adage that "running down people is bad for the heart" is small boat wisdom. The best recipe for a joyful holiday for yourself is to provide the best time possible for everyone else on board.

## Passagemaking

Sailing a small boat from one cruising ground to another at the rate of a fast trot often means cruising at night, sometimes for several nights or, in ocean crossings, weeks. As on merchant ships, someone must be on deck or alert for the safety of the vessel; days and nights are divided into rotating work and rest periods for each crew member. Successful passagemaking means added responsibility for the skipper and mate, and requires organization to arrange watch systems which fit the capability of the crew.

Although for most of us the first twenty-four hours means difficult adjustment to the intermittent sleeping pattern, seasoned mariners slip willingly into the routine, are dependable on watch, and conserve their energy off watch. Novices—especially teenagers—start out bright-eyed and high-spirited, so excited about night sailing that they are up on deck for starlight and moonrise, but they wane with the dawn and are flat out for their next watch. These starry-eyed youngsters should be advised and sometimes ordered to rest in their bunks until they are needed on deck.

For the safety and consideration of off-watch sleepers, give them the quietest part of the boat—the leeward side of a heeling sailboat unless the weight distribution is critical to the speed and progress of the vessel, and employ bunkboards in rough seas. Tone down the deck singing, boisterous laughter and unnecessary vocal diversions which funnel down into the cabin in stereophonic splendor.

Passagemaking is an elemental life; the boat and crew are dependent upon the whims of wind and weather; performing unaccustomed tasks at erratic hours is physically demanding. On the bonus side, however, are rosy-fingered dawns, moonrise, wheeling stars —serenata just for you—and as a fourteen-year-old watchmate observed to us, "It's all free!"

## Offshore Voyaging

Whether to test our maritime skills, or the attributes of our boat, or just because the sea is there, we seafarers suffer an insanity that takes us out of the gentle harbors into the unpredictable oceans. For many of us, this is the time to really test our knowledge, to explore new places, to live with the sea. To supplement the passagemaking information, here are some specifics for offshore cruising:

Show all crew members the location and operation of boat safety gear and deck lights.

Locate safety harnesses, foul weather gear and appropriate deck clothing for ready use.

Team novices with experienced watchstanders.

Check the compass occasionally to be assured that the helmsman hasn't been mesmerized into a course change.

Keep knives, flashlights, cookie tins, radios and other metal objects that may cause compass deviation away from the compass.

Arrange the meal schedule to coincide with the change of watch. If two sittings are necessary, keep the lone watchstander company—it is disheartening to leave the lonely cockpit for a solitary meal.

Avoid prolonged happy hours; many boats offer a tot of whiskey, wine or beer before dinner, often the only time when everyone is together. Others prefer to wait until the anchor is down.

Make available to the crew between-meal snacks and beverages; label out-of-bounds supplies which you need for planning regular meals.

# 7. Shipkeeping

"Six days shalt thou labour,
and do all that thou are able,
And on the seventh,
holystone the decks and scrape the cable."

This weekly pattern was necessary to maintain the beautiful sailing ships of the 18th century in "Bristol fashion." Modern boat construction has changed all that; pride in your vessel and a few hours of loving care each week will keep her in the tradition of the early square-riggers.

## Daily Cabin Care

Galley—Clean sink, counter, stove area; wash, dry, and stow dishes, glasses, and cutlery after each meal (rogue waves may flip dishrack and contents onto the cabin sole).

Cabin—Brush bunk cushions; damp-wipe counters, table top; brush and damp-wipe cabin sole; empty ashtrays.

Head—Clean sink and counter; damp-wipe sole; clean and brush marine toilet, using a small amount of detergent or disinfectant. *Never* use caustics or abrasive cleaners. *Never* put oil, kerosene, or alcohol in the bowl or pump, as these agents cause damage to the valves.

## Occasional Cabin Care

Ports—Wash with fresh water, using a clean sponge and chamois; salt water, harsh cloths and brushes will scratch plastic.

Bulkhead—Wash with fresh water and detergent to remove salt, soot, handprints; rinse with fresh water and wipe dry.

Stove—Remove burner grates to clean priming cup and burners; clean pan under stove; brush burner nozzles.

Ice chest—Clean and deodorize with baking soda and water.

Unpainted wood surfaces—Clean and protect unfinished wood surfaces with cleaner/sealer.

Bunks—Clean under cushions; air bedding on deck (secure well against the wind), and exercise restraint in public places to keep your boat from looking like a gypsy camp.

## Baking Soda

We give top billing to this humble product; it combines all these qualities (also characteristic of the perfect mate): ecological, natural, versatile, and economical. Aboard a boat, some uses of baking soda are:

Galley—Fire extinguisher. Cleans and deodorizes ice chest, cutting board, counters, and drains. Sweetens and removes stains from coffee pot, cups, plastic-ware, vacuum bottles. Dissolves and emulsifies baked-on food and grease from stove and pans.

Head—Deodorizes counter, sink, drain, toilet.

Personal use—Antacid, dentifrice, deodorant, relief from insect bites; sprinkle on washcloths, dish towels and sponges to deodorize. Neutralizes seasickness odor. Layer bottom of ashtrays to extinguish cigarettes and purify.

An inventory of recommended cleaning supplies appears in Appendix D.

## Laundry

Solving the laundry puzzle aboard a small boat takes wit, ingenuity, and, with a Santa Claus pack of ship's washing, a strong back. Every cruising area presents a different problem; here are some solutions of other seasoned sailors.

Supply several sturdy laundry bags, one set for boat linen, one set for clothing. On long cruises with few stops, and when conservation of the boat's fresh water supply is necessary, explain tentative laundry schedules to the guests or crew so that they don't use the fresh water for personal laundry. On long sea passages in fair weather, clothes may be washed in a deck bucket using sea water and liquid detergent and dried on deck (secure well); salt water rinsing produces a clean but salt-soaked garment which retains moisture on damp days. Sturdy articles such as jeans, towels and sheets may be tied to a line and trailed astern, a satisfactory lazy solution (also shark bait).

In port-to-port cruising, most harbor towns have public laundromats with washers and driers. When this facility is available, sort garments for color and heat resistance, empty pockets, bring a pocketful of change

and the laundry detergent ashore and let that strong
foredeck hand tote that bale. It is wise to stay with the
task to prevent the clothes from overcooking in the
dryer and from possible theft. Total time for most boat
laundry (which includes slow-drying jeans and towels)
is 1½ hours—a very boring "time out." Read a book, or
chat with the other washerwomen/men; this is the
place to update your knowledge of the area—where to
buy fresh fish, who sells homemade bread and pies and
what all the neighbors are doing this season.

In some remote areas and in many foreign countries
which have no laundry facilities, it may be possible to
find a local townsman who will take the laundry home
for washing. Drying conditions are chancy, and sometimes total recovery is too. Among people living in true
poverty, the concept of a yachtsman as a millionaire
tempts them to keep for themselves a coveted garment
which they think you may not miss.

Commercial laundries sometimes give twenty-four
hour service; make a duplicate list and establish in advance the estimated bill. We had the shock of the season
on the cold and stormy island of St. Pierre where we
were presented with a week's supply of passagemaking
workclothes for our crew of five—everything folded like
heirloom linen, still warm—and a bill for $45. To de-
liver the clothes in the promised period of time they had
stayed up all night to iron everything dry. If you have
never worn knife-pleated long johns, you haven't really
lived.

# 8. Heavy Weather

"When the sea hog jumps,
Man the pumps."

The dolphin of this old Nova Scotian couplet is just one portent of stormy weather at sea. Changes in barometric pressure, wind shifts, cloud formations, sea bird behavior, and the miracle of satellite weather forecasting can also signal impending storms. Unless you park your boat in your garden, you will at some time have storm conditions at sea, and the first time is a sobering experience. But there are precautions which you may take to keep you calm, your "house" in order, and free you to help on deck if you are needed.

## Storm Readiness

If you are prone to seasickness, take a remedy immediately.

Close and dog all vulnerable ports and hatches.

Have foul weather gear and sea boots in readiness for the deck crew.

Stow all loose gear—especially cameras and spectacles—in a safe place.

Pump the bilges.

Check the stove fuel and fill if needed.

Have safety harnesses and deck lights in readiness for deck crew.

Remove from remote or inconvenient lockers any canned foods or other staples you may need for the next few meals.

Prepare yourself for a long stint in foul weather pants and boots. This garb, incidentally, is excellent protection against burns when cooking in a seaway.

## Cooking in a Seaway

When you have equipped your galley properly for sea conditions, you needn't eat slumgullion—it is possible, and necessary, to serve simple, hearty meals to the hardworking deck crew. If chronic seasickness plagues you, assign the galley task to someone who has a stronger stomach; this will free you to go up on deck where you will probably feel better and can be useful. It is no crime to suffer motion sickness, but it is a sin to starve the crew.

A respectable one-dish meal may be heated on a sea-swing stove without constant tending. This is a slow method—if the fuel is canned heat, *very* slow—so allow plenty of time. When using a gimballed stove, attach braces or retaining rods to hold the pots securely in place. While cooking and serving in rough seas, you will be safer and more efficient if you remain strapped in a

safety harness, passing dishes to a helper near the table or to each crew member in turn. Serve the beverage separately from the main course, unless the dining table is equipped with *very* secure cup-holders, or the diners have three hands. This is no time for elegant table settings and gourmet experiments.

Here are some tips for heavy weather cooking:

Serve a simple one-dish meal—no highly flavored unidentifiable melanges, no runny gravies.

Cut meat and vegetables into bite-sized pieces.

Butter bread or rolls sandwich style.

Place dampened dish towels or paper towels on tables and counters to help keep dishes from sliding off.

Serve half portions of food and liquids in deep mugs or bowls and replenish; don't serve anything scalding hot.

*Never* attempt deep fat frying.

To prevent contents from spilling and overflowing, use deep pots to heat and cook all food and liquids.

Keep the galley sink clear, or have a well-secured deep plastic dishpan ready to receive used dishes and cutlery.

Wash and stow dishes and utensils after each meal.

Be considerate of the crew members on watch, who may need fortifying snacks or beverages while on deck.

## Stormy Weather Menus

All hot dishes in this list may be prepared with simple or canned ingredients and may be cooked on a Sea-Swing stove.

**BREAKFAST:**

Quartered orange sections, tomato or grapefruit juice, dried prunes.

Hot cereal (raisins may be added) served with milk, brown sugar.

Eggs—boiled firm but not hard; scrambled (in double boiler or other deep pan).

Corned beef hash.

French toast or bread toasted in frying pan.

Coffee, tea, or cocoa.

## LUNCH:

Hearty soup—add less liquid than directed to canned varieties.

Pilot biscuits.

Sandwiches—use hard rolls, crusty French bread or firm bread filled with peanut butter, sliced meat, or cheese. Grilled cheese is a five-star special.

Apples, bananas, other firm fruits.

## DINNER:

Stew, creamed chicken/turkey—served on minute rice or Chinese noodles.

Corned beef or roast beef hash.

Ham cubes with sweet potatoes.

Celery, carrots cut in large sticks.

Sea toast, French bread, bread sticks.

Baked beans with cut-up frankfurters.

Coffee, tea, milk.

Apple sauce and gingersnaps, brownies or other cookies.

## SNACKS:

Bouillon, tea, coffee, cocoa, beer, soft drinks, vegetable juice, grapefruit juice.

Fruit cake, fruit cookies, brownies, peanut butter and cheese cracker sandwiches.

Fruit.

Cheese cubes.

Hard candy—sour lemon or orange balls, peppermint
   sticks.
Chocolate bars.

## Living on Your Ear

Weathering a gale at sea on a small boat is an exhausting affair. You will need all your strength, patience, and stamina to perform the simplest cabin tasks.
Above all, you must consider your own safety. Move
with deliberation in the cabin, using handrails at all
times—one hand for you, one hand for the ship is the
rule. Carefully hold and secure locker doors to keep
them from slamming against a hand or foot with the
lurching motion of the boat. Keep the companionway
clear to provide a passage for the navigator and deck
crew, and to allow adequate ventilation in the cabin.
Novices are drawn to the steps of the companionway,
the dry protected seat with a view—this is a lubberly
practice and should be out of bounds for the cook, too,
unless it is necessary to hand up food and gear to the
cockpit crew.

All sleepers should use bunkboards, even in leeward
berths of a sailboat, for their protection in rolling and
pitching seas.

Finding an out-of-the-way home for wet foul weather
gear and boots is almost impossible on a small boat.
With festoons of wet clothing on each surface and the
tired owners in every corner, the cabin combines the
charms of a refugee camp and Chinese laundry. The
seagoing house is a mess. In moments like this I wonder
why I signed on for this kind of madness and why I'm
not home planting tomatoes. You too may have reserva-
tions about the enchanting sea life in these conditions
. . . but then, come morning clearing when the clothes
are dry and you all gather for coffee and tell the saga of
the storm, it's a bright new world that you wouldn't
trade for anything.

# 9. First Aid

A textbook published by the American Red Cross describes first aid as "the immediate care given to a person who has been injured or suddenly taken ill." On land, this care is usually temporary because medical advice is just a telephone call away. At sea, the treatment is the same, with this exception: you may not have immediate professional help. This charges you and the captain with the continuing responsibility for the safety and well-being of the patient. You must know what to do, and even more important, what *not* to do.

To prepare your boat for an unforeseen medical emergency, carry an up-to-date, well-equipped first aid kit and instruction book, and know how to use them promptly and competently.

# First Aid Kit

The size and contents of your medical chest will vary with the extent of your cruising. For short trips in protected waters, you need only the simple supplies which stock your home medicine closet; for offshore cruising and ocean racing, you will need more complete self-sustaining medical supplies. You may buy prepackaged first aid kits at drugstores and marine supply stores, or you may prefer to pack your own container with supplies which are familiar to you or specifically recommended by your physician. All medicines should be well-labelled and stored in waterproof containers to be readily available to you or the crew in an emergency. Plastic fishing tackle boxes, available in hardware and sporting goods stores, make excellent containers for this purpose.

Warning: Many boat accidents occur during commissioning and decommissioning. Your medical kit should be first on, last off.

# First Aid Books

The American Red Cross, for a very modest price, publishes two excellent illustrated books which should be included in every boat and home medicine locker. *Advanced First Aid and Emergency Care* contains advice on the identification and treatment of illness and injury; *Cardiopulmonary Resuscitation* is a small text describing for the layman the current techniques for restoring respiration and circulation to a critically ill victim. To supplement these books, you may also keep aboard one of the nautical first aid books* which deal specifically with maladies common at sea. To be properly prepared for any emergency, read the books *before* starting your cruise.

*The Yachtsman's Guide to First Aid Afloat* by Earl B. Rubell, M.D. (Ziff-Davis Books, New York).

# Prescription Drugs

Offshore racers and deep-sea cruising boats carry prescription drugs to provide more complete care for a crew member who may suffer an accident or illness far from land facilities. If one of your crew members has professional training, he should be consulted about the selection of drugs needed to treat infection, pain, seasickness, and other potential emergencies. A layman should ask a physician to select the medicines necessary for the trip. Store all prescription drugs in waterproof containers, marked for specific use and dosage; some drugs have a limited storage life, especially in damp sea conditions, and should be updated before they have lost their usefulness. Stow these drugs away from the reach of small children. For their safety and to avoid any possibility of misuse of these medicines, I prefer to keep them in a locker separate from other pharmaceuticals.

The investment which you make for these supplies is insurance against calamity. More likely will be the need to care for these very common complaints at sea: constipation, seasickness, and sunburn.

# Constipation

Constipation is an ignoble but frequent accompaniment to the first days aboard; the ailment is caused by inactivity, change in daily routine, and the lack of privacy on a small boat. It is generally temporary, but can be uncomfortable and embarassing to the sufferer while it lasts. Serve natural cathartics, such as bran, prunes, and prune juice, or a mild medical cathartic before the afflicted crew member starts to jog on deck. Another solution which is effective—and undignified— is an abdominal exercise known as "bumps and grinds." It is precisely that, a new accomplishment to keep you awake and healthy during your solo trick at the helm.

Warning: Never give a laxative to a patient suffering symptoms that might indicate appendicitis.

## Seasickness

Cold, hunger, weariness, excessive celebration, lack of ventilation, and strong odors of food, fuel or exhaust are contributing factors to the onset of seasickness. The malady is caused by a malfunction of the balance mechanism of the inner ear. This is not a mental attitude—the victim is *truly* sick. Fortunately the problem is usually temporary and can be avoided or partially controlled by safe medication, and after several days of adaptation to the boat's motion, disappears entirely. Symptoms are weariness, disorientation, lightheadedness, and nausea. A patient suffering a mild case of seasickness recovers best in fresh air, away from engine fumes, galley odors, and tobacco smoke. A forward-facing position on deck with an unobstructed view of the horizon may speed his recovery. A seasickness remedy taken in time should restore him to normalcy in 30 to 45 minutes. Ginger ale or cola at room temperature may be given to a seasick patient in small sips at first, then in gradually increasing amounts if he is able to retain it. Dry crackers or other non-fatty foods may be added as he recovers. Don't force food—the victim probably knows best what is best for his own recovery.

More serious is the care of the victim who suffers continuous vomiting, and, as a result of being unable to retain food or liquids, becomes increasingly weak and dehydrated. This person may be chronically seasick and should cruise under limited, controlled conditions or not at all, out of consideration of others who must attend to him during these moments of strife. And strife it is when in stormy weather one crew member is out flat and another stands out of watch to play nurse. The lee rail is not a suitable place for a weakened patient; move him gently into a prepared lower berth with towels and bucket at hand and stand by to help if he needs assistance with removal of clothing and trips to the head. In a quiet, prone position in the bunk, he may be able to retain a sedative or seasickness remedy, but should be watched to insure his safety if, in a disoriented state, he should rise quickly and fall. If the victim suffers continuous vomiting, and cannot be taken ashore, it may be necessary to administer a lubricated sedative and seasickness remedy rectally.

Warning: Reactions to antidotes for seasickness are unpredictable—some patients are not sick but become drowsy and are not competent to perform all boat tasks. Do not prescribe for young women who may be pregnant; some medications are injurious to the unborn fetus.

## Sunburn

Carelessness, vanity, and ignorance of the burning power of the sun's rays at sea can result in severe burning of the exposed skin, sometimes serious enough to ruin a boating holiday. The only true remedy is to *avoid* the malady by using these precautions: restrict exposure to short periods of sun time until you are acclimated, wear a wide-brimmed hat to protect your face, wear a long-sleeved shirt and pants when swimming and snorkelling in tropic waters, cover feet, apply sunblock to exposed skin.

Warning: Severe sunburn may occur on hazy overcast days at sea. Some expensive "sunning" creams contain only emollients and offer no protection from burning rays.

## Common Cold

Rarely does a cold originate at sea; it is usually contracted on shore, and, in the close informal confines of a boat, can spread to other members of the crew. To prevent contagion, scald all cups, glasses, and eating utensils.

## Special Medications

You should be aware of any routine medicines such as anti-coagulants, insulin, and nitroglycerine which a guest or crew member may be taking, in the event that he suffers an accident or becomes ill on board.

## Alcohol

In the days of the square-riggers and until recently on modern naval vessels, an English seaman received a ration of rum each day, a custom which seemed not to detract from the efficiency of the fleet and must have made for a merry crew. Many of us on smaller craft continue to uphold the fine tradition—and we're a merry crew. However, indiscriminate use of alcohol is dangerous. Poor judgment and unsteady gait on a moving platform can cause injury; the euphoria of an alcoholic helmsman can put the boat in trouble. Dole out the grog in small portions, or wait until the anchor is down.

## Drugs

Anyone using drugs for kicks has no place on a small boat. Moral judgments aside, certain drugs such as cannabis (marijuana) are illegal in the U.S. and other countries. Seaport officers who are trying to control smuggling of illegal drugs by boat traffic conduct thorough inspections of incoming vessels and crew. The penalty for such an offense can be extreme—jail without bail for the culprit, and confiscation of the vessel, *regardless of the innocence of the owner.* Be wary of taking as crew unknown vagrants who are "working" their way from port to port.

# Medical Emergency Aboard

Treat a victim of severe accident in this order:

1. Restore breathing. *Seconds* are important. Treatment may be started immediately even if the patient is still in the water.

2. Move the victim to a safe area *only* if necessary.

3. Remain calm, keep your voice low, and if the victim is conscious, reassure him; you are treating the whole person and his mental attitude is important.

After administration of immediate care for the patient, you will have time to assess the situation. If it is possible to reach shore to aid a critically sick or injured person, conduct the boat as swiftly and *comfortably* as possible to the nearest place for professional help. In offshore waters, without any radio aids, you will use the information in your first aid books and emergency drug kit to the best of your knowledge until you have access to professional help.

# Radio Aids

Citizen Band (C.B.) radios will transmit and receive messages to a distance of 30 to 45 miles in favorable conditions.

Very High Frequency (V.H.F.) radios will transmit and receive emergency messages on Channel 16 within a maximum distance of 100 miles.

# 10. New at Crewing

Lucky is the duckling that emerges from its shell ready for life afloat or the human mariner who has known sea skills from childhood. Also lucky is the would-be sailor who has had an opportunity to learn the ways of the sea by crewing on someone else's boat. Although the contents of this book are directed toward the mate, the information will be useful to you if you are a novice boat guest or crew member. Here also are some specific tips to help you become a valuable member of the crew.

## Pre-cruise Planning

Pack *practical* clothing—consult the inventories in Chapter 4 or ask your hosts for suggestions.

Wear (or pack) deck shoes with nonskid soles for maneuvering on wet decks, rocking dinghies, and slippery docks. Remove hard-soled shoes when stepping aboard to avoid damage to decks and varnished wood surfaces.

Pack your gear in a foldable duffel or packsack (a pillow slip or laundry bag will do). Hard suitcases have no place on a small boat.

For self-sufficiency, carry drugs and pharmaceuticals for your needs for the length of the cruise.

Bring a present for the boat—home-baked goods, a bottle of wine or other contributions to ship's stores are always welcome.

Understand *clearly* instructions for meeting the boat —time, location and alternate plan in the event of delays.

Arrive on time. You may try to telephone if you are unavoidably delayed but keep in mind the unreliability of message delivery in most boating centers.

Bring a paperback book or other expendable reading matter—in our experience sea tales or spy stories make better boat fare than that long-postponed resolve to learn Spanish.

## Shipboard Conduct

Stow your gear in the locker designated by your hosts. Stow *everything* and keep your belongings in the locker when they aren't needed. This compulsive neatness aboard a boat is essential for *your* safety and to avoid damage to *your* possessions.

If you are unfamiliar with the operation of the marine toilet, *ask* for instruction. This is no place for embarassment or experimentation and your skipper or mate is quite accustomed to explaining the mechanics of the head. *Never* put matches, cigarettes, paper tissues (other than toilet paper), sanitary napkins, or tampons in a boat toilet.

Be considerate of others when using the head facilities, especially in the general early morning awakenings.

Conserve the boat's fresh water—washing, shaving, or brushing teeth under a running tap is wasteful.

Observe and remember exact stowage locations and galley practices. My not-to-be-asked-again crew washes the dishes in a creative carefree manner and floods the ice chest with soapy water, while my sail-forever-with-me pals put the knives and forks and spoons in the proper slots.

Help with the cooking, table-setting, dishwashing, and boat-cleaning. My never-again guest entertains the cockpit gang with travelogues of the Orient while I juggle dinner, but my any-time-you-need-a-berth chum makes the lunch sandwiches and leaves the galley spick-and-span.

During boat maneuvers, if you aren't familiar with the procedures, stay clear of more experienced crew members. The skipper will tell you where to stay and will ask for your help when it is needed.

Observe and remember the maneuvers in order to be a participant in the future.

Don't be a chatterbox (a Bermuda racer I know calls it verbal diarrhea), especially during course-plotting, sail-changing, docking and undocking, and anchoring.

## Liberty

Shore leave is time for fun and games, but do offer to tote the laundry or help with the marketing on your way to the bright lights.

If you are rich, invite your hosts and shipmates ashore for a meal.

If you are poor, dig clams for supper, pick berries for breakfast, or buy a few inexpensive surprises for the galley stores.

With these reminders tucked under your watch cap and the charm and talent that brought a cruising invitation your way, you will be a welcome addition to any boat, for this trip and many more to come.

# 11. Cruising With Children

It's the last day of vacation and the wind has piped up to 25 knots—right on the nose, and by pounding all day and through the night you might be lucky enough to get home tomorrow for work and dentist appointments and household commitments. The skipper is under pressure and ill-tempered; the children are tired and frightened; the mate is in tears. Sad end of family holiday and sometimes, end of family cruising. This is a familiar theme —don't let it happen to you. Probably the most common mistake in planning boat vacations with children is trying to pack in too many experiences and cover too great a distance in a short time. Family cruising should be *fun*. You can make it fun by planning a flexible schedule with lots of time out for swimming or shore adven-

ture. You may go no farther than the next harbor, but you all will have a joyful holiday.

Start your cruise with a "director's meeting" (everyone is a director) at home and let everyone consult the charts and guide books to help plan the cruise, list gear to pack and create menus for the trip. Discuss safety rules before you start, to keep the holiday from becoming a week of vetoes.

On board, let each young crew member be responsible for some boat task, rotating the jobs so that everyone may follow the drudgery of garbage disposal with the glory of course-plotting. Cooking and meal-planning are creative projects for any age. The best Scottish shortbread we have ever had was tenderly hand-blended and watchfully baked by our fifteen-year-old foredeck hand.

## Safety Rules for Small Fry

The importance of establishing safety practices for shipboard living with small children can't be overstated. Anyone who has been a witness or participant at a waterfront tragedy or near tragedy involving the young can never be casual about this aspect of family cruising. Spare yourself worry and heartbreak by establishing sensible precautions and by following them *always*.

All nonswimmers should wear life jackets on deck, in the dinghy, and on docks. Ignore the protests of your young who admire the free-wheeling, unguarded, unjacketed four-year-old of Family X. Modern flotation vests are available in all sizes; they are lightweight and allow mobility for the most active youngster.

Shipboard swimmers should be supervised, especially from the boat ladder, where there may be danger from water skiing and small outboard

traffic, or where strong tides and currents may carry
even the most competent swimmer away from the
boat.

Supervise the use of the dinghy to keep a pleasant row
from becoming a misadventure in the event of the
loss of an oar or following a shift in wind and tide.

A youngster who is old enough to go ashore for a long
solo foray should have a good understanding of the
geography of the area, and should carry a watch,
compass, flashlight, and firm schedule for return-
ing to the vessel.

## Games and Diversions for Family Boating

To many adults, just being on board a boat is complete
enchantment. The very young may need a little more
entertainment to satisfy their lively curiosity and
matching metabolism.

Shipboard days, especially the long daylight hours of
summer, can seem endless to a small child. Let each
youngster bring aboard a suitable shipboard project of
his own choosing. You too should have a small supply of
"surprises" for days of rain or glassy calm when bore-
dom and the fidgets begin to interfere with family fun.
Knot-tying and macramé are good boating pastimes.
Soap-carving from floating Ivory bars can be sophis-
ticated sculpture by teenagers, or simple renditions
(with the use of safe plastic knives) by the younger crew
members. Try kite-flying and soap bubble pipes by day,
or star-finding and story-telling at night. Night can be
concert time; bring along any musical instruments for
which you have talent (and space aboard). Play card
games, checkers, chess, backgammon, Scrabble. Try
memory games, fortune-telling, charades. Let everyone
write a Haiku poem, limerick or skit based on life at
sea.

Some kind of food preparation is within the capability
of everyone. A four-year-old can prepare a salad; a six-

year-old can make sandwiches. On rainy days try fudge, popcorn, cinnamon toast, top-of-the-stove gingerbread.

For most youngsters, a good leg stretch is a necessary balance to the relative inactivity of boat living. Plan an "off-boat" project in every cruising day. A promised swim before lunch will insure cooperation by the small fry in sail-changing and anchoring. Let them help to con the boat into a harbor, douse the sails, rig a swimming ladder, and make lunch while you have "Time Out." If it isn't convenient to anchor, and weather and sea conditions permit safe swimming from the boat, let the young crew douse sails and rig a ladder and safety lines. This "middle of the ocean" swimming is high adventure. A vigilant adult should stay aboard during this time.

End of the day anchorages are often protected waters for sailing or rowing a dinghy and possibly trolling for fish for supper. On beaches which are open to the public, we all are Robinson Crusoes. What treasures have washed ashore this day? What sea creatures live in the tide pools? There may be clams for supper or blueberries for breakfast. (On these land forays, you will be well advised to inspect the vegetation to be sure that there will not be poison ivy for the rest of the week.)

Bring the frisbees and waterproof soccer and volleyballs ashore. On the beach, build sand castles and sand sculpture with prizes to be awarded later in the day. Play follow-the-leader, fox-and-geese, leapfrog. Run. Swim. Dance. And respect the rights of all by leaving behind nothing but your footprints.

Seaport exploring is fun for everyone. Feast on ice cream. Hike. Rent bicycles. Let each child shop for an inexpensive surprise to share with the rest of the crew at suppertime.

Car travel games can be adapted to boating life. Can you identify each boat by its hull shape or sail motif? How many foreign ports on the transoms of passing boats can you list? Which boats have the prettiest

names? The craziest? Design the boat of your dreams—
or the funniest.

There are endless possibilities for entertainment for
you all. There are new adventures, new places, and a
new way of life to expand the knowledge and imagina-
tion of your children—and with thoughtful planning—
new family unity. Use these hints, invent more of your
own and enjoy happy family cruising.

# 12. The Personal Equation

An important base for successful life at sea is a well-found boat. Just as important is the partnership with a good skipper. In the course of establishing a pattern for cooperation, there are triumphs and pitfalls—up the slippery ladder two rungs, down one. As in every business partnership, love affair, or marriage, success doesn't happen overnight. Also, the immediacy of the decisions sometimes required to maintain boating safety may present stresses which are never encountered in shore life.

The first step in setting up a working team is to recognize that these stresses exist, that captain and crew, skipper and mate face a tough taskmaster— the sea— whose fine today, fickle tomorrow moods makes exhausting demands of all its followers. There will be ex-

tremes of wind and weather, and you will be bone-weary from small-boat living in these conditions. It will be nerve-wracking to the skipper too, and harsh words may fly—sometimes directed your way. Many mates-in-training have quit here. However, if you can accept these temporary aberrations as such, and not end of the world calamities, you have made a big step toward teamwork with your skipper.

With full knowledge that there is a debit side to boating life, why does a woman forsake her home sanctuary for the inconveniences of a small boat? Most of us join the marine world because we love the sea. We love its challenge and beauty and grandeur. Many of us join the boating scene because our skippers have fallen in love —with a boat. It is no coincidence that the vessels are named *Psyche, Juno, Circe, Aphrodite, Mistress,* and no secret that the owners lavish time, attention, and money on them. If we first mates are wise enough to welcome these ladies, not to fight them but to join them, we enter into a ménage-à-trois in which everyone comes out a winner.

## Role of the Skipper

A boat certainly benefits from the care bestowed upon it by a team. What are the advantages to the skipper? First, he has a partner to share the responsibility of cruising, someone who can relieve him of some of the physical work load, and who is able to return him, and the boat, to safety should he become incapacitated. Most valuable to him is the presence of a close companion who enjoys an exhilarating sport, and who will join him in the evening gam at the end of a boating day.

Although the skipper's side of a boating partnership is weighted by the responsibility of command of his vessel, he should wear his captain's cap with modesty. A familiar complaint of cruising mates is that a skipper who is full-fledged angel at home turns into a despotic devil on a boat.

Here are some hints for the thoughtful skipper to help the mate in her boating training. For efficient teamwork in a complicated boating maneuver of docking, undocking, sail-changing, or anchoring, times when speed and accuracy are vital, discuss in advance the steps for executing the operation, and assign tasks which suit the capability of the mate. Respect the physical limitations of crew members, particularly women, who may not be able to wrestle down a flaying jib or handle a heavy anchor. Unless emergency conditions demand loud commands, use a clear, *quiet* voice for your instructions, and leave out the pseudo-salty vulgarity which the *Naval Officer's Guide* describes as the "crutch of an inadequate vocabulary." If it is necessary to correct the mate or crew member, do so privately away from others. Remember to praise a job well done. If *you* have goofed, swallow your pride and admit it. Every captain who has followed the sea has at some time made a miscalculation or blunder and it is no blot on your record to join the ranks.

## Role of the Mate

The role of mate, although subordinate to the skipper in making final decisions, demands knowledge of every aspect of boating. As second in command, the mate not only supports the skipper's plans, but must be capable of making decisions in an emergency.

Where does the job of captain stop and yours, as mate, begin? Ideally, they are interchangeable. You should know how to operate everything on board your boat. This assumes that you have the ability to tackle any task from navigation to electrical engineering; if you have these qualifications, you are probably president of your own large company and need no advice from anyone.

For a less-than-genius mate, the following suggestions should guide you in your part of the boating team.

You should know the location of the mechanical systems of your boat and understand their functions well enough to be able to recognize efficient performance, or to diagnose a malfunction. Unlike the secretive placing of electrical wires, plumbing pipes, and jacketed furnace in a house, these fittings on a boat are conspicuously placed and fundamental enough for comprehension by a curious five-year-old, let alone a clever mate like you.

The fresh water system aboard most small boats is a miracle of simplicity. You will become familiar with the water intake fitting, usually located on deck, because it may be your responsibility to oversee the filling of the tanks to make most efficient use of the time your boat is alongside a gas dock. Safety shut-off valves close the intake and outlet hoses when the boat is not in use. Hand pumps or, in a pressure water system, faucets deliver the water to the galley sink or head basin—and that's all there is to it. A pressure system is only slightly more complex, so welcome to the world of marine hydrodynamics.

Similarly, you should know enough about the boat engine or auxiliary to recognize smooth performance or malfunction, and you should be able to identify engine parts well enough to assist in making repairs, if necessary. If your dinghy is equipped with an outboard motor, you should be capable of operating it and making simple adjustments, replacing a spark plug or shear pin in an emergency. Although engine maintenance has been traditionally male-oriented, I know many women who excel at this trade, and some who are number one mechanic on board their boats.

If you have no strong talent in mechanics, you should at least be familiar with the below-deck workings of the electrical panel, battery system, safety valves for fuel and water, marine toilet operation, and electronic gear such as depthfinder and radio direction finder. Just as you can identify the familiar clicks and hummings of home appliances, so you will soon be aware of boat sounds to detect smooth functioning of the apparatus or potential trouble. In many instances, women have the nose (or ear) for trouble, and you may find that you are the one who first smells unfamiliar fumes or hears a laboring motor, acute detection which may save costly and time-consuming breakdowns later.

Cabin maintenance is your bailiwick. Along with the normal task of monitoring the supply of fuel for the galley stove, cabin lamps, and heater, you should be able to free sticky pump valves, trim wicks, and clean burners.

On deck, you must understand a myriad of boat fittings—and the nomenclature. A "thimble" is not to protect your sewing finger, a "sister-hook" is not for grappling with your sibling, and a "jigger" does not a martini make. You should be able to apply seamanlike whipping to the ends of docking lines and sheets, and to repair sails. Sewing skills will stand you in good stead on a sailboat. My finest racing record was spent on the foredeck of a sailboat, sewing one end of a mammoth rip in the #1 jib while the skipper's wife worked from the other, a non-stop marathon of stitchery that was completed just in time for re-setting the sail at the next mark.

Akin to sail repair, but more creative, is square-knotting or macramé. A pastime of early sailors on long ocean passages, this almost dying art has been revived by young craftsmen, and is the perfect handiwork project on board a boat. Macramé decorates and protects bell pulls, hand grips, ships' wheels, winch handles, boat hooks, and swabs, and after the boat has been garnished, there can be belts and bags for the skipper and crew. Of the many instruction books on square-knotting, *The Ashley Book of Knots* is *the* encyclopedia. It is a treasure trove of boating lore and well worth a few moments of your time to enjoy your link with the seafarers of clipper ship days.

Expert helmsmanship is a skill which cannot be learned overnight. Very frustrating to the beginner is the first trial in docking and maneuvering a craft which has shown complete cooperation in the hands of an expert, but which, in less experienced hands, becomes a stubborn maverick. Learning to judge proper speed and distance is a matter of practice—and *more* practice. In time, you should be capable of steering your boat in all sea conditions; you must also be able to steer by the compass, using and acknowledging changes in the boat's course by using the correct nautical terms.

Just as local law and highway guides control the safety of automobiles, maritime Rules of the Road determine rights-of-way at sea. These regulations are respected by every capable mariner and should be at the top of the list in your boating knowledge.

Night cruising adds a fillip of mystery to boat life, and also an element of risk. To maintain safety at sea in night conditions, each vessel must show prescribed lights so that it may be easily identified by another craft. Lighted channel markers and beacons mark safe waters or hazards. Piloting a boat through this Christmas tree confusion after dark requires good judgment and fast reactions, and may involve the concentration of everyone on board. Even then, total cooperation may not always solve the puzzle of lights at sea. Directly in the path of a small sloop racing along the shore of Chesapeake Bay, two uncharted flashing channel markers appeared, and, just short of panic by the crew, rose gracefully out of the water. Mystery solved—a midnight seaplane in full flight.

Piloting and navigation, traditionally the responsibility of the captain, are skills which require accuracy, not muscle power, and can be learned by any woman who has the interest and time to devote to this part of boating. However, only a few men or women have the necessary aptitude, opportunity and dedication to practice and become experts in the field. A proficient navigator is much in demand. A talented and beautiful Canadian contemporary spends every summer piloting small sailboats along the rocky fogbound coast from Nova Scotia to New England. She brings the tools of her trade aboard in two small boxes—one for her trusty sextant, the other for her shore-festivities wig.

Although you may never become this super-tactician, you should be able to intrepret a chart, plot a course, and understand the buoyage system of the waters in which you plan to cruise. Nautical charts are the road maps of the sea. Published by the National Oceanic and Atmospheric Administration (NOAA) of the U.S. Department of Commerce, charts of the U.S. waters are beautiful to behold and comprehensive in their information. They are invaluable to every yachtsman, fisherman, and ship's navigator—and to *you*. If you can read a cookbook or interpret a bank statement, you can learn to read a marine chart. Study the mapped area in which you are cruising each time you are aboard to become familiar with the symbols and abbreviations which identify hazardous areas or safe waters for your craft.

Actual piloting—plotting and interpreting a compass course—is the next step. The subject of piloting is covered well in elementary courses offered by the U.S. Coast Guard Auxiliary and the U.S. Power Squadron. If you cannot attend their classes, ask your skipper or some other knowledgeable navigator to give you a step-by-step work session with theory and practice. Record the facts in your boat notebook, and practice when you are aboard. As you become more competent, you will be able to guide your craft with safety and efficiency. You will also develop a sixth sense for the elements which surround you. Without mechanical instruments, you will feel wind shifts on your face and note an increase or drop in boat speed; you will be aware of tide or current changes, recognize changes in color or motion of the water to differentiate safe depths from shoal, and notice wind and cloud patterns that indicate changes in the weather.

## Anxieties and Antidotes

Newcomers to boating may experience fears and worries which seem inconsequential to experienced mariners. To a novice, the pitching and rolling of a small boat in moderate seas, or the heeling aspect of a sailboat, are not exhilarating sport but out-of-control dangers. Fearful of falling overboard or of being trapped in a capsized boat, unschooled in sailing and boating theory, and ignorant of the safety features of good boat design, the rank beginner is off to a poor start when the wind pipes up and the pleasure craft to him becomes a torture chamber. Reassurance by a knowledgeable seaman who recognizes these fears as real (and temporary) is a first step toward helping the learner gain confidence in the ways of the sea. If you, the learner, are uneasy in rolling waves while your shipmates are singing in exultation on your "walloping windowblind," heed the explanations and demonstrations which will free your worries and put you back in the chorus.

Briefed in theory and attuned to the motion of a boat at sea, the mariner-in-training soon loses fear for her own safety. She may, however, have a more deep-seated worry about a boating emergency which would incapacitate the skipper or crew members, leaving her with responsibilities which are beyond her knowledge and training. This is a concern which afflicts experienced mariners—one which many of us never outgrow. Although we have never lost a crew member overboard in our many years of sailing, I still worry. Better than fretting over potential accidents, though, is planning a course of action which will enable you to deal with the emergency coolly and competently.

# Man Overboard

Of course you are well-trained in the use of lifesaving gear aboard your own boat; be just as knowledgeable of the emergency equipment of every boat on which you cruise. You don't need to make a big production of your interest, but you should note the location and release mechanisms of safety gear aboard every boat. Sea rescues are best controlled under power. Know the procedure for starting and operating the boat engine or auxiliary, and also the location of fuel shut-off valves and safety devices which may impede prompt action.

Much study has been given to the subject of sea rescue. The drama is recorded in poetry, prose, and song. Current documentaries and articles record explicit descriptions for rescuing a victim from the water. Learn the theories, but, better still, put the theories into practice. Treat a jettisoned paper cup or blown-away cap as your "victim" and try to effect a rescue expedition, as though the floating object were human. Conduct a man overboard drill on a calm day, in waters which are relatively free of boating traffic, by jettisoning a life cushion or some other floating object. Use this as your target and bring the boat to it in a simulated rescue procedure. This practice game is a good test of your competence in a real emergency. It can also be a sobering experience, as I discovered on my first trial, when I performed a rescue of my large straw hat. My first pass was a wide circle which wasted precious minutes, and landed me five boat-lengths from the hat; next, I bravely gathered speed and ran the "victim" down; on the third try, I succeeded in bringing aboard the damp and battered head-gear, thanking my lucky stars that it wasn't the skipper. (Strangely enough, he has never gone overboard for a test of the real thing.)

However awkward my first trial, I am confident now that I could maneuver a boat properly, and I have a mental plan of action, should I be faced with a man overboard situation. Very briefly, my general course of action would be: jettison lifesaving gear, cushions, any flotation objects at hand; start the engine and free all sails; note the compass course and read the reciprocal; turn to the reciprocal course or follow the path of floating objects until the victim is in sight; approach the victim into the wind, and slowly; when he is alongside, rig a temporary line to which he can cling until a swimming ladder or any other device for helping him aboard can be set. Lifting a heavy, exhausted man from the water, a difficult task for a strong crew member, may be an impossible one for a woman. If you plan to cruise shorthanded in offshore waters, I recommend that you and your skipper devise a rig, suited to your strength and your boat design, for bringing a victim safely aboard in an emergency.

Every able seaman carries a knife on board a boat. Clipped to my belt by a lanyard, my stout little stainless steel knife is used as often to spread peanut butter as to repair boating gear, but it is always at hand for an emergency should I need it. If you invest in this indispensable aid, buy one that you can open and operate quickly. Some rigging knives and jackknives are real nail-busters, and require brute force to open.

## Communication

Outdoor sports inspire us to raise our voices to their full decibel level—appropriate for the cheering section of a football team, but inconsiderate to the occupants of other boats and shore houses in a quiet anchorage. Clarion calls from bow to cockpit carry the length of the boat, and the length of the harbor. A small cove forms an acoustically perfect amphitheater, and, unless you wish to entertain the entire fleet, it is good practice to tone down your directions and responses.

Even better is the use of hand signals between helmsman and foredeck crew. During our anchoring procedures, we find that hand cues are easy to interpret and lead to fewer misunderstandings than the hoot-and-holler method of communication. Our signals are simple: a beckoning hand means to come ahead, a clenched fist is stop, and the hitchhiker's gesture is the cue to back the boat. In uncomplicated anchoring conditions, the entire maneuver can be conducted without a word spoken. During trickier maneuvers, hand signals keep unnecessary chatter to a minimum.

Silence is golden. But, silence is worth diamonds in those boating situations which require concentration by the skipper, and coordinated action by his crew. In our exuberance, we crew members are apt to keep the conversational ball rolling when it might better be put to rest. A thoughtful first mate can be most helpful by knowing when to call attention to potential hazards, and when to be silent.

## Psychology and Common Sense

Courtesy counts. In creating a smooth-functioning boat team, good manners are as important to successful partnership as knowledge of the sea. We all admire the boat in which skipper and mate work in perfect harmony; unfortunately, we also witness boats in distress, the skipper shouting orders and the mate in tears. There are those theorists who malign this captain, interpreting his abusive behavior as latent belligerence, with the boat as his weapon and the mate his intended victim. Perhaps such skippers exist, but I don't know them. My belief is that any mariner who yells and bellows at his mate, does so in helpless frustration at a sport which taxes his every physical and intellectual resource. These are stressful times for him and for the recipient of his fury. *He* must learn to curb his emotions, if he is to become a respected seaman, and she, in return, can help him by holding *her* critical tongue.

Neatness also counts. Close proximity in boat living

requires keeping everything in its place. The first time you step into someone else's deck shoes because they were left by your bunk is comic—the ninth time is not. A considerate mariner keeps personal gear stowed away when it is not in use.

In teamwork practice, everything counts. Habits and modes of behavior which may be mildly irritating ashore can become the source of enmity aboard a small boat. A King's Point maritime cadet described his secret for adapting to new companions in the close quarters of a ship by stating that he "never made any waves," advice which I wish I had been wise enough to follow in earlier days.

While learning things the hard way, I have created some monumental "waves." For example, the shared ice chest/chart table, covered by carefully plotted charts and other navigation gear for an imminent harbor entrance, is not the place to arrange the appurtenances for afternoon tea. Another example: an engine overhaul, with the boat cabin in shambles and the skipper in fits, is not the time to receive visitors from the neighboring boat.

Skippers have not been fault-free either. In a docking situation which calls for line-casting beyond the capabilities of a pitcher for the Yankees, jokes about the throwing ability of women are not in good taste. Also, in the final ministrations to a wet and balky stove burner, demands for chipped ice and the makings of a bloody mary are distinctly unwelcome.

There will be times which will tax your patience too. Teamwork requires work from all of us. Use your good manners and good sense, and keep *your* team together.

# 13. Time Out for the Mate

"What do you *do* on a boat?" ask the land-based chums. Surrounded by your admiring crew, you lounge on deck in the sunset to exchange tall tales of the sea over tall tinkling drinks. Yes, there will be some of that —but to properly round out the picture, you will also: buy and cook food for at least 21 meals a week for that faithful crew; transport mountains of laundry and supplies to and from the shore; scrub every visible and hidden surface of the boat; repair zippers, pot handles, saucepans; stitch torn spinnakers, ensigns, sneakers, jeans; coil and uncoil miles of line; bag and unbag acres of sail. You are chauffeur, charwoman, commissary officer, cook, tinker, tailor . . . sailor . . . all those wizards.

Satisfying the challenges of boating life may take all your energy and perhaps more time than you had an-

ticipated on your seagoing holiday. You need a few hours for yourself, by yourself, freedom that is hard to arrange within the confines of a small boat. Unless you revel in the role of galley slave/martyr, you must schedule time out—time for indulging in your own projects, worthy or frivolous. Read, nap, embroider, sing, play your recorder or guitar, polish off the Sunday crossword, do your nails, tan the back of your legs, write a poem, sketch the harbor scene, deck the boat with McNamara's lace, photograph the fleet. Remember to bring aboard your hobby materials or books. The quality of supplies and reading matter in many small ports is often tasteless or nonexistent.

Your well deserved time out may be worked into the boat schedule more easily if you *share* the boatkeeping and galley chores. Let your guests or crew polish up the old brass lamp—or stove—or cabin sole. Cooking in someone else's kitchen is a lark. Let the others produce a gourmet specialty; it's time out for you and a chance to learn new galley tricks. The surrogate cook deserves the same breaks that you do: a free companionway, counter clear of electrical repairs or other engineering creativity, and exemption from dishwashing and cleanup.

Long associations in close quarters may fracture the tender structure of crew compatability. The jolly laugh becomes a cackle, jokes pall, casual chatter is a bore; earrings in the coffee cup, foul weather gear on your bunk are pushing you to the brink. Time out for the mate—time to go off alone (or with the pal of your choice). If it is impractical or inconvenient to make shore liberty, take a sail or row in the dinghy, swim around the harbor, or spend a lazy hour on the foredeck. Just a little time out will deflate your bubble and make you able to enjoy the companionship of your shipmates again.

Sometimes the skipper/mate relationship has come unstuck. You absentmindedly let the bilge pump run for an hour and the captain welcomed you to the society of mechanical clods and dumbbells; for the twentieth time he didn't wash the engine oil out of your best saucepan; you have rigged the jib sheet inside the rigging *again;* why can't he take that blasted pipe out of his mouth so you can understand his docking instructions? Et cetera. A small boat with others aboard is not the place to hold a tribunal which will be uncomfortable and embarassing for everyone. Take time out together to settle your differences—chances are that a few hours together may be what you both have needed to return to cheerful partnership.

Crew changeover during a cruising holiday is a hectic time. Departing guests are developing withdrawal symptoms as they pack and plan their return to the "real world." Meanwhile, in come the new crew members, full of bounce and high expectations. Between the two, if you have allowed time for a breather, you still must fit in the necessities of laundry, boat clean-up, marketing, and personal upkeep. Sometimes you have a grand overlap of homebound crew and new arrivals, each with duffel, foul weather gear, shopping bags and shore shoes; add a few garbage bags (outgoing) and grocery cartons (incoming); sprinkle with salt spray from the overburdened dinghy or the gentle dew from heaven, and you have cause to consider taking time out for the rest of the season.

We all have differing levels of patience and varying degrees of tolerance for boating discomforts—a situation that is comic relief to you may give me a raging headache. Fortunately however, the moments of frustration are few and fleeting, and I will allow no more self-indulgent commiseration and soul-searching, because ours—the world of boating—is the best of all worlds. Each distressing memory for me is far overshadowed by recollections of these glorious places and joyful adventures.

Les Isles de la Madeleine—entering Havre Aubert with the pre-dawn scalloping fleet, followed by celebration for all hands. Our 14-year-old son was introduced to some pretty dubious yachting habits—caviar, smoked salmon, and bloody marys before sun-up.

Whitehead, Nova Scotia—sitting in a sunny meadow with my new 12-year-old friend and namesake, Margie, and sharing her family's berry patch—blueberries in our pockets, raspberries in our straw hats, a mélange for on-the-site tea.

Matinicus, Maine—after a bouncy three-day passage, morning ablutions with my shipmate Jan, naked as jaybirds in a waving shoreside kelp patch.

Alanya, Turkey—captively sequestered in the steaming tourist information office by the bandit-faced agent, who in apology for his lack of English delivered an hour-long violin concert, interrupted only by thimbles of tea and his soulful sighs.

Chesapeake Bay—a plethora of ethnic diversions in San Domingo Creek, drinking Irish whiskey in an orange Hallowe'en moonrise with my only comrades—my Scottish skipper and 600 Canada geese.

Gulf of Maine—celebrating Independence Day with said skipper riveted to the helm in a midnight electrical storm which offered a two-hour son-et-lumière, hot rain, and icy hailstones—the Fourth of July spectacular of all time.

Most important to me is the companionship of cruising shipmates, friends and crew, their husbands or wives who have shared the fine sights and great adventures, and without whom, this book could not have been written:

> Harriet and Ruth—co-owners and co-skippers of our 19″ Cape Cod Knockabout and partners in the summers of zany Long Island Sound cruising; Jo—mentor and supervisor of my graduation to "big boat" cruising; Scotty—racing instructor with commands as soft as a sonnet; Gretchen, waking for her night watch like

a smiling angel; Dilys, co-adventurer in shore treks and haunted houses; Simon the cherubic buccaneer, Tom, the romantic balladeer. Also, the bounties of Bill's outrageous puns, Roberta's witty quips, Kay's sea-cookery, Jean's ocean-crossing expertise, Teedie's cabin artistry, Townie's eagle eyes, Bob's helmsmanship, Barb's champagne fetes, Don's folk songs, Sarah's seamanship, Ben's ebullience. Not to overlook the literary chums, Carolyn and Alice; Charlie, the philosopher; Horace, the other arctic swimmer, Chazz, number one crew.

Last in mention, but first in the list, is my skipper husband—friend and fearless navigator—who has charted us through tens of thousands of miles of fresh water rivers and lakes and open oceans on all manner of vessels from 14′ canoe to live-aboard yacht, who has shared his patience and humor and sea lore—and who shares a life-long addiction which I hope to pass along to you Mates—a love of the sea.

# Appendix A
# Recommended Table and Cook Ware. Dishwashing Supplies

## COOKING EQUIPMENT

Constant exposure to salt and dampness is hard on boat gear. Buy the best that you can afford; it is wiser to start out with a few pans of good quality than a kitful of second-rates. All metal items should be stainless steel or aluminum. Measure the surface of your boat stove—particularly two-burner models—before buying griddles, frying pans, and teakettles to be certain that the cooking units will accommodate several large vessels.

| BASIC COOKWARE | EXTENDED COOKWARE |
|---|---|
| Teakettle (4 qt.) | All basic cookware plus: |
| Frying pan (10′)* | Frying pan (12′) and lid* |

*Highly recommended for boat use are frying pans with durable non-stick inside surface.

Saucepan (2 qt.),
double boiler and lid
Saucepan (small) and
lid

Coffeepot
Griddle
Lobster cooker
Dutch oven
Cake pan to fit inside
Dutch oven
Pressure cooker
Toaster (stove top)

# GALLEY IMPLEMENTS

BASIC

Serving spoon
Slotted serving spoon
Small cooking fork
Spatula
Tongs
Whisk
Can opener
Bottle opener/corkscrew
Ice pick
Pliable scraper/spatula
Carving knife
Paring knife
Serrated vegetable knife
Wide blade spreading
knife
Potato parer
Kitchen scissors
Spare key for fish and
meat tins

EXTENDED

All basic implements
plus:
Wooden spoon
Salad knife and fork
Eggbeater

# TABLE CUTLERY

BASIC

6–8 knives
6–8 forks
6–8 dessert spoons

EXTENDED

All basic cutlery plus:
6 steak knives
6 lobster forks

|                    |                    |
|--------------------|--------------------|
| 8–10 teaspoons     | 2–3 lobster crackers |
| Serving spoon      | Butter spreader    |

All boat cutlery should be nonrusting stainless steel.

## DISHES AND GLASSES

**BASIC**

**EXTENDED**

6–8 dinner plates
6 deep cereal/soup bowls
6–8 mugs
6–8 stacking glasses (small)
6–8 stacking glasses (tall)
2 mixing bowls (small, medium)
Platter (wood or plastic)
Tray (wood or plastic)
Wooden ice bucket
Sugar bowl and lid
Pitcher

All basic tableware plus:
Butter dish
6–8 dessert plates
6–8 juice/wine glasses
Vegetable serving bowl
Cheese board

Because of unavoidable breakage conditions on board a small boat, plasticware is preferable to fragile glass and china; even then, it is wise to buy a few extra pieces for replacement when the pattern is not reliable open stock, and may be discontinued.

# OTHER GALLEY AIDS

BASIC

EXTENDED

Flame-shooter and
extra flints
Matches (in water-
proof container)
Funnel (for potable
liquids)
Funnel (for stove and
lamp fuels)
Heatproof tile or pad
Potholders
Ice tongs
Ice bags
Timer
1–2 plastic juice pitchers
with lids
Plastic containers for
leftovers
Salt and pepper shakers

Juicer
Measuring spoons and
cup
Meat thermometer
Strainer
Placemats (nonskid)

# DISHWASHING EQUIPMENT

Plastic dishpan to fit inside sink (the roll of the boat
often causes water to drain out prematurely).
Plastic dishpan (to hold dishes and utensils *after*
washing during rough sea conditions).
Dish towels (fast-drying).
Brush, sponges, pot cleaners.

# APPENDIX B
# FOOD STAPLES, PAPER GOODS, AND SUNDRIES

Rarely will a small boat carry *all* of these food supplies unless planning long offshore or ocean crossing passages. Keep a notebook record of the items which best suit your cruising practice.

## DRY STAPLES

Bouillon—powdered instant dissolves more quickly than cubes

Cereals—Wheatena, oatmeal; compact cold cereals such as Muessli, Grapenuts, Shredded Wheat

Cocoa or powdered chocolate drink mix

Coffee—instant as well as ground

Cornmeal

Crackers

Cookies
Flour
Lemonade crystals
Macaroni, noodles, spaghetti
Milk—powdered skim
Mixes—biscuit, cake, gingerbread, muffin, pancake
Nuts—salted, unsalted
Potatoes—dehydrated
Popcorn
Raisins
Rice
Salt
Soups—dehydrated
Sugar—brown, confectioners, white
Tea

# BOTTLED STAPLES

Chutney
Honey
Jam and jelly
Ketchup
Maple syrup
Marmalade
Mayonnaise
Mustard
Oil
Olives
Peanut butter
Pickles
Relish
Salad dressing
Tabasco
Vinegar
Worcestershire sauce

# CANNED FOODS

The availability of fresh and frozen foods has caused some of us to overlook the excellence and variety of canned products; experiment with different brands at home so that you may stock your boat with quality foods of superior flavor and little waste. These canned foods have proven to be most versatile and popular on our boat.

Fruits—apples, applesauce, cherries, cranberry sauce, fruit cocktail, peaches, pears, pineapple

Juices—cranapple, grapefruit, prune, tomato, V-8

Soups—black bean, celery, chunky soups, chicken, clam chowder, consomme, mushroom, pea, scotch broth, tomato

Vegetables—asparagus, beets, bean salad, carrots, corn, onions, peas, potatoes

Baked beans

Fried rice

Chinese noodles

Brown bread

Puddings—Indian, butterscotch, chocolate, lemon, plum

Bacon

Corned beef

Corned beef hash

Chicken chunks

Ham

Meat spreads

Turkey chunks

Crabmeat

Shrimp

Salmon

Tuna

# HERBS AND SPICES

Basil
Cinnamon
Cloves
Curry powder
Garlic powder
Ginger
Lemon pepper
Marjoram
Meat tenderizer
Nutmeg
Onion flakes
Pepper
Pepper flakes
Tarragon
Thyme

# CANDY

Chocolate—fudge mixes make good rainy day cookery
Hard candy—sour lemon, orange
Lollipops
Peppermint sticks
Sesame candies

# BEVERAGES

Beer
Soft drinks—Reserve and stow separately a small supply of *naturally-* or *sugar-sweetened* ginger ale or cola to administer to seasick victims to prevent dehydration
Alcoholic drinks
Mixers

# PAPER AND OTHER WRAPPING PRODUCTS

Aluminum foil—heavy
Paper cups and plates
Paper napkins
Paper tissues
Paper towels—more than you think that you will use; these go fast on a boat
Plastic garbage bags—medium size for boat trash container and large size for accumulated trash
Plastic bags—small and medium sizes
Plastic wrap
Toilet paper
Wax paper

# SUNDRIES

Candles—with *safe* holders for dining table; birthday candles
Charcoal briquettes
Clothes hangers
Garment bags
Insect spray
Matches
Rubber bands, string, twistems
Writing paper, pads, pencils, pens, waterproof markers

# Appendix C
# Recommended Health and Pharmaceutical Aids

Note: The items listed here are *in addition* to the supplies in your medical first aid kit.

Ace bandages
Alcohol (for external use)
Analgesic cream (for treatment of sunburn and insect bites)
Antibiotic cream (for cuts and wounds)
Antacid tablets
Aspirin
Band-Aids
Constipation remedy
Comb (spare)
Cotton-tipped swabs
Cough lozenges

Dental floss
Deodorant
Diarrhea remedy
Eye drops
Ice bag
Insect repellent for skin
Lighter fluid (or other spot removal agent)
Lotion (moisturizing for face and skin)
Meat tenderizer (for treating jellyfish sting)
Petroleum jelly
Powder (for body)
Powder (fungicidal)
Razor (spare)
Salt pills
Sanitary napkins and belt (and tampons)
Seasickness remedy
Seasickness bags (airline variety)
Shaving cream
Soap
Splinter kit
Sterile pads
Sunburn cream (protective and blockout)
Toothbrush (spare)
Toothpaste
Towelettes

# Appendix D
# Recommended
# Cleaning Supplies

## CLEANING SUPPLIES

Abrasive powdered cleaner (in plastic container)
Anti-mildew agent
Baking soda
Brass and copper cleaner
Clothespins
Detergent (mild for
dishwashing)
Detergent (laundry)
Detergent (strong for cleaning)
Deodorizer
Disinfectant
Wood sealer and cleaner (for
untreated surfaces)

Abrasive pad (for cleaning galley
pots)
Brush and sponge (for dishwashing)
Brush (for marine toilet)
Bucket (separate from deck bucket)
Chamois (for cleaning ports)
Rags (for general use *and* for the
engine room)
Scrub brush
Sponges (for general cleaning)
Swab
Toothbrush (for impossible corners)
Whiskbroom (for bunk cushions)
Whiskbroom and small plastic
dustpan (for cabin sole)

# Glossary

**Aft** Stern or after end of a boat
**Below** Below decks
**Bilge** Lowest point of a boat's inner hull
**Block** Pulley
**Bow** Forward part of boat
**Bowline** Sailor's knot which forms a loop that will not
    slide or jam
**Bristol fashion** Shipshape, kept in trim like the ships in
    Bristol, England
**Broach** To veer in a following sea, causing a boat to lie
    sideways to the waves
**Bulkhead** Wall, partition of a boat
**Bunk** Built-in bed
**Bunkboard** Safety extension of side of berth.

**Cable** Wire rope or strong chain for securing anchor to ship

**Cleat** Wooden or metal fitting around which a rope or line may be made fast

**Clove hitch** Sailor's knot securing line at right angle around post

**Cockpit** Area surrounding helmsman's station

**Companionway** Stairway or door leading down into cabin

**Compass** Instrument for determining direction

**Con** To direct the course of a boat

**Deviation** Deflection of the needle of a compass, caused by local magnetic disturbance on the ship

**Dinghy** Small rowboat used as tender

**Ditty bag** Small bag used to hold string, needles, thread

**Dog** Mechanical device for clamping or securing hatch; to clamp hatch

**Dorade** Deck ventilator directing air into cabin

**Dory** Flat-bottomed boat with high flaring sides for off-shore fishing

**Downeaster** Resident of Northeast U.S. or Canadian Maritimes

**Eyebolt** Sturdy bolt with ring at end

**Fathometer** Instrument for measuring depth of water

**Fender** Protective buffer between boat and dock to absorb shock and prevent chafing

**Fiddle** Protective lip at edge of table or shelf to keep articles from sliding off

**Fo'c'sle** Forward of the mast; living quarters for sailors

**Fore** Front part of boat

**Foredeck** Forward part of deck

**Foul weather gear** Waterproof storm jacket and pants

**Galley** Boat kitchen

**Gam** Friendly visit or conversation among sailors

**Gimbal** Device for keeping apparatus level or on horizontal plane

**Hatch** Opening in deck for access to cabin

**Head** Marine toilet

**Heel**  To list or tilt to one side

**Helm**  Steering apparatus; wheel or tiller

**Holystone**  To scrub a deck with sandstone

**Hook**  Anchor

**Jigger**  Small after sail of a ketch or yawl

**Ladder**  Boat stairway

**Landlubber**  One unacquainted with the sea

**Leeward**  Away from the direction of the wind

**Locker**  Boat cupboard or drawer space

**Lubberly**  Unseamanlike

**Mark**  In racing, a buoy or other object indicating a turning point

**Mate**  Deck officer on merchant ship ranking next below the captain

**McNamara's lace**  Decorative ropework or macramé

**Mug up**  Drink or between-meal snack

**One-off**  Individualized one-design boat

**Overhead**  Boat ceiling

**Painter**  Line used to secure or tow a small boat

**Port**  Left side of boat facing forward; window of a boat; harbor

**Sail-stop**  Tie for securing furled sail

**Saloon**  Living or dining area of a boat

**Seaway**  Moderate or rough sea

**Sextant**  Instrument for making precise angular measurements. Commonly used in celestial navigation at sea

**Shakedown**  Test to familiarize crew with operation of a boat

**Shear pin**  Easily replaceable pin designed to break under excess stress, used to protect propeller of an outboard motor

**Sheet**  Line for trimming sail

**Shipshape**  Trim and orderly

**Shock cord**  Heavy elasticized cord

**Sister-hook**  Shackle formed by two circular clip-hooks

**Skipper**  Captain or master of a boat

**Sloop**  Boat with a single mast

**Slumgullion** Weak drink or soup

**Sole** Floor of cabin

**Sou'wester** Waterproof hat with long brim in front and back

**Starboard** Right side of boat facing forward

**Stem** Timber or support uniting the two sides of the ship at the forward end

**Thimble** Grooved ring which fits into a spliced loop of rope to prevent chafing

**Turk's-head** Tubular knot, largely decorative, worked around a cylinder

**Watch** Sailor's assigned period of duty

**Watch cap** Close-fitting hat worn by sailors in cold and stormy weather

**Whipping** Binding or seizing at the end of a rope to prevent untwisting or ravelling

**Winch and winch handle** Apparatus for hauling in sail

**Windscoop** Above-deck device for directing air below decks